SECRETS OF A
SUCCESSFUL ORGANIZER

A LABOR NOTES BOOK

SECRETS OF A SUCCESSFUL ORGANIZER

ALEXANDRA BRADBURY
MARK BRENNER
JANE SLAUGHTER

A LABOR NOTES BOOK

Copyright © 2016 by Labor Education and Research Project

First printing: March 2016
Second printing: September 2016
Third printing: May 2017
Fourth printing: January 2018
Fifth printing: October 2018

Reprints

Permission is granted to workplace activists, unions, rank-and-file union groups, and labor studies programs to reprint sections of this book for free distribution. Please let Labor Notes know of such use, at *editor@labornotes.org*, 718-284-4144, or the address below. Requests for permission to reprint for other purposes should be directed to Labor Notes.

> Labor Notes
> 104 Montgomery St.
> Brooklyn, NY 11225

Cover and inside design: Sonia Singh

Library of Congress Control Number: 2016934473
ISBN: 9780914093077
Printed in Canada

*To all the organizers who never lose sight of
the fact that a better world is possible, and
never stop working to get us there.*

CONTENTS

LESSON 3: MAP YOUR WORKPLACE AND ITS LEADERS

LESSON 4: CHOOSING AN ISSUE

LESSON 5: AN ESCALATING CAMPAIGN

LESSON 6: EXPECT THE UNEXPECTED

LESSON 7: ALWAYS BE ORGANIZING

LESSON 8: PUTTING IT ALL TOGETHER

ACKNOWLEDGMENTS

A book, like an organizing campaign, is a group effort. Though only three names appear on the cover, in truth the rest of the Labor Notes staff helped to write and assemble what you hold in your hands:

Chris Brooks, Dan DiMaggio, Adrian Montgomery, Sonia Singh, and Samantha Winslow.

We're also grateful to those who shared perceptive feedback on early drafts. Their ideas improved the book greatly:

Gene Bruskin, David Cohen, Ellen David Friedman, Joe Fahey, Laura Kurre, David Levin, Matthew Luskin, Peter Olney, and Guillermo Perez.

Most of all, we owe an enormous debt to everyone whose words, experiences, and insights we've included. We drew from many sources, including articles we've published in *Labor Notes* over the years, materials shared by friendly unions and organizations, and our previous books *Democracy Is Power, A Troublemaker's Handbook, A Troublemaker's Handbook 2, The Steward's Toolbox,* and *How to Jump-Start Your Union.*

A huge thank you to the people whose stories and lessons you are about to read, and those who helped us tell them:

Ahmed Ali, Michael Ames Connor, Judy Atkins, Zainab Aweis, Nicholas Bedell, John Braxton, Aaron Brenner, Jenny Brown, Gene Bruskin, Cara Bryant, Carlos Campos, Maria Chávez, David Cohen, Shamus Cooke, Jeff Crosby, Angelina Cruz, Ellen David Friedman, Monica De Leon, Marcela Diaz, Steve Eames, Kay Eisenhower, Matt Ellison, Joe Fahey, Rafael Feliciano Hernandez, Jon Flanders, Katy Fox-Hodess, Chele Fulmore, Mischa Gaus, Julian Gonzalez, Norine Gutekanst, LaKesha Harrison, Adam Heenan, Rob Hickey, Steve Hinds, William Johnson, David Kameras, Patricia Kane, Julia Kann, Dennis Kosuth, Paul Krehbiel, Chris Kutalik, Dan La Botz, David Levin, Luis Lucho Gomez, Matthew Luskin, Dan Lutz, Kathryn Lybarger, Maria Martínez, Ray Martinez, Paul McCafferty, Hanna Metzger, Margo Murray, Greg Nammacher, Seth Newton Patel, Marsha Niemeijer, Ellen Norton, Liz Perlman, Nick Perry, Debby Pope, Sandy Pope, Jackson Potter, Hannah Roditi, Jonathan Rosenblum, Hetty Rosenstein, Shannon Ryker, Charlotte Sanders, Caniesha Seldon, Judy Sheridan-Gonzalez, Kenzo Shibata, Gregg Shotwell, Jerry Skinner, Rick Smith, Bill Street, Tiffany Ten Eyck, Belinda Thielen, Jerome Thompson, Roberto Tijerina, Andrew Tripp, Jerry Tucker, Joe Uehlein, Bess Watts, Jim West, Justin West, Dorothy Wigmore, Laverne Wrenn, and John Zartman.

HOW TO USE THIS BOOK

We've distilled the fundamentals of organizing into 47 secrets and arranged them into eight lessons, each illustrated with real-life examples from *Labor Notes* magazine and our books.

For best results, read together. Organizing isn't a solitary activity. You could read this book alone, but you'll learn more if you talk each lesson over with a buddy—or better yet, a group of co-workers.

Try the exercises. Each lesson includes an exercise or two to help you apply what you've learned in your own workplace. Again, these work best as group activities.

Use the handouts. You might want to hand out certain pages to co-workers, or use them in a steward training. Photocopy whatever you like, but for your convenience, we've made selected materials available for free download, in a letter-sized format that's easy to print and share. All the exercises are included. Get the free downloads online at *labornotes.org/secrets*

 SECRETS   **EXERCISES**

 REAL-LIFE EXAMPLES   **HANDOUTS**

 TIPS

 # LESSON 1: ATTITUDE ADJUSTMENT

You're reading this. That means you're interested in organizing where you work. You want to fix problems you see around you. Maybe something unfair has happened to you, or to someone you work with, and you want to *do something* about it.

For us, that's organizing. For the boss, that's trouble. People who try to *do something*—especially when they bring others together to *do something* collectively—are often labeled "troublemakers."

But we suggest you wear the word with pride. From Mother Jones to Martin Luther King, Jr., the best organizers have been reviled as troublemakers, because they were bringing people together and building strength in numbers that threatened the power of the few.

Organizing is a lot like cooking: there are time-tested recipes that anyone can learn, methods that work and some that don't. Your results may not be perfect every time—since we're dealing with human beings here—but you will do better if you learn from the successes and mistakes of the organizers who've gone before you.

STOPPING HARASSMENT

In a meatpacking plant in Pasco, Washington, management had had its way for years. Conditions were dangerous, floors were slippery, and harassment was a constant. The union was weak; very few members were involved.

But that all began to change when a few workers decided to organize their co-workers to make their work life more tolerable.

One of their first steps was to hold meetings in the cafeteria for people who worked on each production line. Anyone willing to attend could help make plans to deal with their worst shop floor problems.

"The company wasn't happy about the meetings," said Maria Martínez, the chief steward. "They started sending supervisors to listen to us. They said we weren't allowed to hold union meetings in their cafeteria. I told them that the National Labor Relations Act gives us the right to organize and to hold meetings in non-work areas at non-work times.

"Management told me to put it in writing. So I did. I wrote a grievance and had 100 people sign it. That was the last I heard from management about that. And we kept on meeting in the cafeteria."

A common topic at the meetings was harassment. So volunteers on each production line began training their co-workers to document the harassment and encouraging them to stand up to it. Martínez said, "If a supervisor said something, we'd say

Tony Perlstein

real loud to other people on the line, 'Did you hear what he just said?'"

When incidents piled up, members would go as a group to higher-level managers. They prepared in advance to tell their stories, so that one person wouldn't be stuck doing all the talking.

The actions worked. Supervisors—perhaps to avoid friction with their own bosses—started to back off.

To keep supervisors in check, another tactic the workers used was grievance forms, modeled after disciplinary tickets. Workers could "write up" their supervisors by checking off violations. Usually all the people from one line would sit down and document the harassment together. One copy went to the offending supervisor, one to the union, and one to management.

Later you'll read more about how these meatpackers changed their workplace—and dozens of other stories from workers who noticed something wrong and started organizing to fix it.

ORGANIZING IS AN ATTITUDE

Organizing is first of all an attitude. It's the attitude that you and your co-workers together can *do something* to make things better. It's the attitude that action is better than complaining. It's the attitude that problems are just waiting for a solution, and that strength in numbers is part of that solution.

It's the refusal to be discouraged—at least not for long. It's the willingness to listen to others with respect, so that the plan you come up with reflects the good ideas of many people.

If you have the organizing attitude, you feel it is *necessary* to respond to unfairness. You are committed to building power with your co-workers, not just talking about it. You believe in collective action and want to get better at putting others in motion.

THE ORGANIZING ATTITUDE

- Action is better than complaining.

- Problems are waiting for solutions.

- Solutions are collective, not individual.

- People can be brought together to make things better.

ORGANIZING IS FOR EVERYONE

Though this book was written with union members in mind, many of its lessons apply in non-union workplaces, too.

But be careful, especially about acting alone. If you don't have a union, management can get rid of you for a bogus reason, or no reason at all. You'll find more safety—and strength—in numbers.

Consider contacting a union for help. And at the end of this lesson, see the sidebar on your legal rights.

APATHY ISN'T REAL

The first attitude adjustment an organizer needs is to get over the idea that co-workers don't care—that your workplace is bogged down in "apathy."

It's a common gripe. In Labor Notes workshops we often ask union members to make a list of the reasons why people don't get involved where they work. Typical answers include:

- Lack of time.
- Don't know how to do it.
- The union is not open; there's no easy way in.
- Conflicts between groups.
- Conflicts between individuals.
- My co-workers feel that nothing will change.
- They think everyone *else* is apathetic.
- They're looking for individual solutions.
- And the big one: fear.

Sound familiar? It might feel like your co-workers don't care. But push a little bit, and that's never really true.

Everyone cares about something at work. Just about everyone cares about their wages, for instance. Everyone wants respect. No one's indifferent to whether their shift is miserable. It's impossible not to care.

Could it be that your workplace is the one in a million where everything's fine? Maybe your co-workers are completely secure about their jobs, love their supervisors,

Everyone cares about something at work.

make excellent money with terrific benefits, have no worries about downsizing or layoffs, face no health hazards, and are confident about their retirement. If so—put down this book and get another hobby!

But it's more likely that people are scared to say anything, or feel powerless.

They might say everything is fine because they don't believe it can change, or they can't imagine it being different, or they assume the problem they care about isn't a "union issue." Organizing is the antidote.

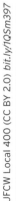
UFCW Local 400 (CC BY 2.0) *bit.ly/1QSm397*

Remember Maria Martínez's co-workers at the meatpacking plant? Most had never been to a union meeting—but they did care that their supervisors were harassing them. They just didn't think they could do anything about it. Once they saw people organizing to tackle the problem, they wanted to get involved.

So when you're assessing why more people haven't stepped up to take on the boss, it's important to find out the actual reasons. You have to diagnose the problem before you can write the prescription.

It's not apathy—but what is it?

You have to diagnose the problem before you can write the prescription.

Step back from your frustration and look at things from an organizing perspective. This chart shows five common problems and how you can help your co-workers get past them:

HOW THE BOSS KEEPS US DISORGANIZED

The boss relies on...	The organizer...	Co-workers find...
...**fear** of conflict and retaliation.	...taps into **righteous anger** about workplace injustices.	...the **courage** and determination to act.
...**hopelessness**, the feeling that things can't change and we have no power.	...helps develop a **plan to win,** and shares examples of victories elsewhere.	...**hope** that change is possible and worth fighting for.
...**division**, pitting workers against each other.	...identifies **common ground** and builds relationships.	...**unity** to act together.
...**confusion**, passing around messages that will alarm or distract us.	...**interprets** and shares information, fitting it into a bigger picture.	...**clarity** to see through the boss's plan.
...**inaction,** since problems can't be solved, so why bother?	...**mobilizes** co-workers to do something together.	...that action gets **results** and solves problems.

Download this chart at
labornotes.org/secrets

WHAT'S THE REAL PROBLEM?

Here are some ways to understand what looks like apathy, and to respond to it.

"No one seems to care."

Everyone cares about something—but the *something* might not be what you expect. Pick out a few co-workers you'd like to know better. Make a point of talking with them, and find out what's on their minds.

Maybe the drug-testing policy that's grinding your gears isn't at the top of their list because something else is bugging them more: a foul chemical in the air, a mean supervisor, a toothache and no dental plan, a shift that means they hardly see their kids, being forced to defend a stupid policy to customers… The only way to find out is to listen.

Someone who's facing sexual harassment, for instance, might feel strongly about it—but she might assume it's not *your* issue, or not a *union* issue.

Show your co-workers respect and understanding. When they feel that from you, they're more likely to respect the things you care about.

"It's hard to see how things could change."

Maybe your co-workers are just as bugged by the drug-testing policy as you are, but it seems too big to

Dan Lutz

tackle. The boss has done a good job of cementing the idea that the decision is final—and fighting it sounds like a waste of time.

It's perfectly reasonable that people feel this way, especially if they've always felt powerless and disorganized at work. People are used to going along to get along. If your co-workers have never *felt* strength in numbers, or seen a group take action to change even something small, why would they believe they could change something big?

As an organizer, it's your job to inspire your co-workers that change is possible if you work together. Part of this is developing a credible plan to win. Ask, "What solution are we proposing?" "Who in management has the authority to say yes?" "What could we do together to get that person to

Look for fights you can win with the people you have on board so far.

say yes?" Share stories of tactics that have worked elsewhere (you'll learn plenty in this book).

Often it helps to start small. Involving your co-workers in a tiny campaign that gets results is a way to "show, not tell" them that collective action has power.

Look for fights you can win with the people you have on board so far, taking just a small step out of their comfort zone. When it works, more people will be drawn in. As they participate, their confidence will grow, and you can go farther each time. (We'll talk more about choosing an organizing issue in Lesson 4.)

Hopelessness can be a strong habit. It's easier to break a habit with group support. Bringing people together can help individuals get past their discouragement.

"No one's willing to do anything."

Have you asked them personally to do something specific? Most of us aren't natural-born organizers. Many of your co-workers won't initiate activity—but they might respond if asked directly by someone they trust.

Figure out some very small, specific requests, and personally approach a co-worker. At first this might be as simple as answering a survey, coming to lunch with other co-workers to discuss a problem, or signing a group letter. (We'll talk more about choosing your tactics in Lesson 5.)

Figure out some very small, specific requests.

Be respectful of time constraints in their lives. Show lots of appreciation for anything they're willing to do—and make it clear that any victories were won by the whole team. This attitude of respect will encourage them to do more in the future.

"No one comes to meetings."

Think about how people are notified about meetings. An email or a notice on the bulletin board isn't enough. Personal, face-to-face invitations are the best. Divide up your workplace and find several other people to share the work of inviting people individually.

Also consider the practical things that could make meetings more accessible: scheduling, location, childcare, translation, transportation.

When people do come to a meeting, it had better be pleasant and productive—or they won't be back! People are incredibly busy these days, and you convey respect for their participation by planning the meeting ahead of time. Prepare a clear agenda, a time limit, and a reason to attend, such as a hot issue.

If a meeting is just to "get information," it's easy to skip it. People will be more motivated to attend a meeting where they have a meaningful role to play— for instance, to help make an action plan. If you miss that meeting, there's a consequence: the plan will be made without your input.

All that said, sometimes people simply can't make it to meetings—for instance, because of parenting responsibilities. These people can still play crucial roles in organizing while they're at work. Be flexible.

Download this at
*labornotes.org/
secrets*

#3 AIM FOR THE BULLSEYE

If you ask union members to draw their union structure, most will draw a pyramid: officers at the top, rank and file at the bottom. Some might get clever and draw an inverted pyramid with the rank and file at the top.

But a better way to think about your fellow members, from the organizer's point of view, is like a dartboard with concentric circles.

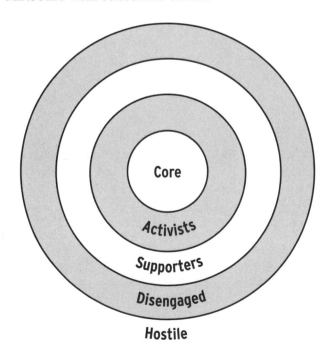

Core

Activists

Supporters

Disengaged

Hostile

In the center is your **core group**: the people (maybe you?) who are always thinking about organizing and how to get others involved, even on their time off. They might be elected leaders or shop stewards, or not.

In the first ring are the **activists** who can be counted on to help when an issue heats up. They will take responsibility to get the word out and will ask other people to take action, too.

In the second ring are **supporters**: people who will wear a button or sign a petition, but don't take responsibility for getting anyone else involved.

In the third ring are the people who appear most **disengaged**. They don't see the union as a factor in their lives, so they don't participate.

There are also people outside the circle who aren't just uninvolved—they're **hostile** to the union. Don't waste your time arguing with the haters. Maybe one day something will open their eyes, but it'll probably be an experience, not a debate, that does it.

EXERCISE:
DRAW YOUR OWN BULLSEYE

Stop and think about where people in your workplace fit into the circles. Can you think of one or two examples of co-workers in each position— the core group, activists, supporters, disengaged, and hostile? Draw a bullseye and write a few names in each circle.

#4

YOU'RE DIFFERENT, AND THAT'S OKAY

Jim West, jimwestphoto.com

It's crucial for the organizer to understand that the concentration of co-workers in the outer rings isn't a sign of failure. Most of your co-workers won't ever become dedicated union volunteers, day in and day out.

Even in winning campaigns, the planning, the strategizing, and a fair share of the grunt work are typically carried out by a handful of members: the core group. The activists and supporters join in as needed, and a lot of the people who are usually disengaged play a part when the stakes get highest—for example, during a strike.

Don't set the bar too high. You can't send a message that to be involved in the union, people have to be like you. They'll shy away. Making a meaningful contribution shouldn't require devoting all their days and nights. Instead, help everyone to find their own levels of involvement. And as you take on different fights, don't be surprised when people move between roles—sometimes acting as leaders, other times hanging back.

A good goal is one activist or steward for every 10 workers.

But you probably do need more people to join you in the core group, and more supporters to step up as activists. "More hands on the plow," as master organizer and Auto Workers rabblerouser Jerry Tucker used to say. Union veterans will tell you that a good goal is one activist or steward for every 10 workers, including at least one on every shift and in every department or work area.

Your organizing task is, how are you going to move more people toward the center of the bullseye? Help them take one step at a time, moving from being disengaged to supportive, or from support to activism, or from activism to taking on core responsibilities. Never make your core group an exclusive club.

#5

DON'T BE A HERO

Sonia Singh

The Lone Ranger was not an organizer.

As an organizer, you can't be a superhero or a firefighter. (Even if you *are* a firefighter.) Your role isn't to knock the door down, burst in, and rescue people; it's to build a team of activists.

Guard against the impulse to put yourself at the center of everything the union is doing. As the great civil rights activist Ella Baker said, we need more movement-centered leaders, not leader-centered movements.

This attitude adjustment can be challenging, since many of us are motivated by a strong sense of injustice. You're outraged at the petty slights the supervisor dishes out. You don't want to let the problem go on a moment longer.

But a good organizer taps into that righteous anger in others, motivates people to take collective action, and gives them the experience of bringing about change together. That's how you build power at work *and* develop leadership.

This is particularly hard because your co-workers often expect you to be the hero. They are comfortable letting you take all the risks. But they won't learn to help themselves—or help each other—if you do everything for them.

So when a co-worker comes to you with a problem, instead of tying on your cape, look for ways you can help her to get the ball rolling herself.

TROUBLEMAKERS CAN'T BE SLACKERS AT WORK

Do your job consistently and do it well. Don't make yourself an easy target for management. Co-workers will respect you more, too. Try to recruit people who are good at their jobs into your core group of organizers.

#6

THERE ARE NO SHORTCUTS

What we need to do is often simple, but not easy. It's hard to carve out time for conversations, really listen, and keep chipping away at obstacles that take time to overcome.

It's often tempting to seize on something that promises quick results. Maybe this new cellphone app will get our co-workers excited about the union! If we start ordering pizza for our meetings, everyone will come! But what sounds too good to be true, probably is.

The basics of organizing don't change. You can't wave a magic wand and instantly get power on the job. That only comes by doing the patient work of building relationships, identifying issues, and running campaigns. As famed organizer Fred Ross put it: "Shortcuts usually end in detours, which lead to dead ends."

Here are a few examples of shortcuts that will work against you in the long run:

- Solving the problem yourself by going to management alone, instead of getting co-workers to come with you.

- Continually relying on the same leaders, instead of developing new ones.

- Shutting down bad ideas, instead of asking questions that help your co-workers realize why the idea won't work—or sometimes even letting them make their own mistakes.

- Using Facebook to "invite" people to a union activity, instead of having a personal conversation.

The Puerto Rican teachers union spent years fostering a culture of democracy, developing grassroots leaders, and forging relationships between teachers and parents. The teachers did it through many small fights, on issues like smaller classes, asbestos removal, school supplies, and water fountains.

All this painstaking spadework enabled the union to strike for 10 days in 2008, in defiance of the law, and then to defeat a raid by a much wealthier union that dumped tens of millions of dollars into the attempt. As President Rafael Feliciano Hernandez put it at the time: "The long way is the short way."

What sounds too good to be true, probably is.

Read more in *Democracy Is Power.*

#7 IT'S ALL ABOUT POWER

Street Vendor Project

In any workplace, the underlying issue is power: who has it, who wants it, and how it's used. Power is "the whole ball of wax," says Hetty Rosenstein, who headed a local of public workers in New Jersey for many years.

Read more in *A Troublemaker's Handbook 2.*

Yet many people are uncomfortable with power. They find it hard to talk about, and are reluctant to seek it. People shy away from the conflict and unpleasantness it implies.

"People want to believe that if we're fair and we're brilliant, then we'll get what's right," Rosenstein observes. "But it isn't enough. You can't just empower yourself. You have to take it away from management."

Organizers need to understand what makes it hard for people to push for power. Then you can help them take the first step.

When training Chicago teachers to organize their co-workers, organizer Matthew Luskin starts with a discussion of power: What is it? Is it good or bad? Where does it come from? Who has it?

He asks, what would we do if we had all the power in the world? The group brainstorms a list: "Affordable housing for all." "Free health care." "No more wars." "Education instead of prisons."

Without warning, Luskin slips into a role play. He writes "POWER" on a piece of paper and holds it up over his head. "Well, this is a nice list that you all made," he tells the group, "but I have all the power, and I have a few issues with it…"

> **Organizers need to understand what makes it hard for people to push for power.**

Channeling a corporate executive, politician, and obnoxious supervisor rolled into one, he starts ridiculing their list and crossing things off. "Health care? All you have to do is pay me for it. I own some great insurance companies and hospitals." "Why would I want free higher education?" "Well, this one is ridiculous…"

Luskin can carry on this tirade indefinitely. He won't stop until a group of people stands up, chases him down, and snatches the paper labeled "POWER" out of his hands.

People figure out pretty quickly what's going on. Often someone pipes up to say, "We all need to take the power from him!" But still, it's usually a long time after that before people get up the nerve to do it.

Afterwards they talk about why it took so long. People were embarrassed. They didn't want to look stupid. They were afraid of being the first one to act. They weren't sure other people would back them up.

These concerns are universal—and, Luskin emphasizes, they're perfectly reasonable. Fighting for power is risky and uncomfortable, especially at first. What gets people through it? Having a plan, seeing someone else take a risk, and finding safety in numbers.

SEEK OUT MENTORS

As your organizing takes off (or runs into roadblocks), you'll soon need individual support and feedback from an experienced organizer. If you're in a union, try asking your local staff or officers for help. In some locals they'll be thrilled to hear from you, and a great resource. If not, look elsewhere.

Labor Notes events are terrific places to meet organizing mentors—that's part of why we put them on. Also try Teamsters for a Democratic Union or your local Jobs with Justice coalition. Call our office and we'll do our best to put you in touch with someone near you who can help.

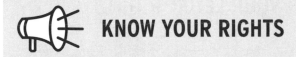 # KNOW YOUR RIGHTS

Justin West worked at the Mitsubishi factory in Normal, Illinois. He tells how he and his co-workers "spoke truth to power."

After one area of the plant went through a week of blatant contract violations by managers, workers talked about strategies and settled on a plan. One night on second shift, a majority of the workers in the area taped 8½ x 11 signs to their backs, bearing messages such as:

- 'Pride'
- 'Respect'
- 'Dignity'
- 'Stop Walking on the Contract'
- 'I Have Rights'

Upper managers got wind of it within minutes, and demanded that the signs be removed. The workers protested and held their ground. Labor Relations was called down.

After 20 minutes of battling, management threatened disciplinary action against everyone. The workers did remove their signs—under protest—but notified management that Labor Board charges would follow.

The next day, the union received a settlement in its favor on one of the major grievances the workers were protesting, short-notice mandatory overtime.

YOUR LEGAL RIGHTS TO ORGANIZE

It's helpful for an organizer to know what protections you have under U.S. labor law. Enforcing your basic rights can be a good way to show your co-workers that the boss isn't all-powerful. The law is not a silver bullet; some of its protections and penalties are weak, and court cases can drag on for years. Still, it's an important tool in your kit.

Often you don't have to go to court to enforce the law. Simply knowing and asserting your rights can have a powerful effect. Remember the meatpacking plant described at the beginning of this lesson? Managers objected to union meetings in the cafeteria, but workers knew the law was on their side. After 100 people signed a grievance saying so, managers backed off.

ON THE JOB

Most private sector workers' rights on the job are protected by a federal law, the National Labor Relations Act. (It doesn't cover agricultural workers, domestic workers, independent contractors, or supervisors. Airline and railroad workers are covered by a separate, similar law, the Railway Labor Act.)

Concerted activity. The NLRA protects your right to engage in "concerted activities for the purpose of collective bargaining or other mutual aid or protection"—in other words, to take action with at least one other person to improve conditions at work.

Protected concerted activities include filing grievances, complaining about contract violations, holding rank-and-file meetings, visiting the boss in a group on non-work time, petitioning, wearing buttons, and other ways of pressuring the boss. You have these rights whether or not there's a union at your workplace.

Download this at
*labornotes.org/
secrets*

Management or union officials may not harass you by spying on you or interrogating you about rank-and-file meetings or other protected activities. Neither your employer nor your union may lawfully discipline you for exercising your rights.

Bargaining and strikes. Some rights are different depending on whether or not you have a union. In a

WHAT IF I WORK IN THE PUBLIC SECTOR?

If you work for the government, you're not covered by the NLRA unless you're a Postal Service employee. But most public employees are covered by federal or state laws modeled on the NLRA.

You can find the law for federal employees at *flra.gov/statute*, and the state laws at *bit.ly/ StateUnionLaws*.

Government workers also have free speech protections under the First Amendment if they are speaking about matters of public concern. That's in addition to any union contract protections.

union workplace, the employer is obligated to bargain with the union and to answer information requests. There's no such obligation in a non-union workplace.

On the other hand, non-union workers have the right to strike at will—though this is taking a big risk. Union members are usually bound by contract language not to strike till the contract expires.

Distributing literature. You may distribute leaflets at work in non-work areas, on non-work time. Non-work areas include the parking lot, the time clock, the cafeteria, or anywhere people go on break outside the work area. Soliciting signatures on a petition may be done in working areas on non-work time as long as no literature is passed out.

You may use company-provided, general-use bulletin boards to post literature and notices. If workers can post things like cartoons, event flyers, or order forms for Girl Scout cookies, it's a general-use board. Rules that forbid posting union-related literature, or that the boss creates in response to union or rank-and-file activity, are illegal.

> You may distribute leaflets at work in non-work areas, on non-work time.

The National Labor Relations Board (NLRB) may allow employers to prohibit the distribution of literature that criticizes the employer's product or services in a way unrelated to labor issues, if the primary target of that literature is the customer base or general public.

Workers' Action Centre

Online. Internet conversations between co-workers—such as Facebook posts, tweets, or blogs—get the same protections as face-to-face conversations about wages, hours, and working conditions.

If your rights are violated, you may file a charge at the NLRB. If the Regional Office decides your case has merit, it will schedule a hearing and provide a lawyer to prosecute it. Your charge must be filed within six months of the date your rights are violated.

But remember, the wheels of justice turn slowly. When in doubt, think like an organizer, not like a lawyer.

IN THE UNION

If your union includes private sector workers, your rights inside the union are protected by the Labor-Management Reporting and Disclosure Act. (If your union represents exclusively public sector workers, the laws vary by state.)

Free speech. You have the right to meet, organize, and speak freely. Union officials may not disrupt rank-and-file meetings or distribution of literature. You have the right to speak at union meetings, subject to reasonable rules (such as Robert's Rules of Order).

Elections. You have the right to an equal opportunity to vote, nominate candidates, and run for union office. You have the right to a secret-ballot vote on increases in local union dues, initiation fees, and assessments.

Contracts. You have the right to receive, upon request to your local, a copy of your contract, and the right to inspect all contracts that your local administers.

Union financial statements. Every private sector union must file an annual financial statement with the U.S. Department of Labor containing officer salaries and expenses and other union expenses and income. The report, known as the LM-2, LM-3, or LM-4 (depending on the union's size), is a public document and can be obtained online at *bit.ly/UnionSearch*.

Defending your rights. Unfortunately, the law is nothing more than words on paper unless you can enforce it. A great resource for actually enforcing your rights is the Association for Union Democracy. Visit its website at *uniondemocracy.org*.

The purpose of this lesson was to help you take a deep breath and get your head on straight for the organizing tasks ahead of you. In the next lesson we will explain the very foundation of organizing. It's an activity that comes naturally to many but that makes other people's knees quake: one-on-one conversations.

Whether you're a "people person" or not, you'll find that it's the personal touch that makes all the difference—and we'll learn more about that in **Lesson 2: One-on-One Conversations.**

LESSON 2: ONE-ON-ONE CONVERSATIONS

Now that you've learned about the bullseye model, maybe you're breathing a sigh of relief that your workplace is not the most "apathetic" on the planet.

But how do you find out which issues your co-workers care about, and which obstacles are holding them back? How do you encourage more of them to move from disengaged to supportive, and then to active, and then to joining your core group of organizers?

It's simple: you talk with them.

GETTING TO KNOW YOU

Rochester-Finger Lakes Pride at Work

In Rochester, New York, civil service worker Bess Watts learned the importance of one-on-one conversations after she decided to found a local chapter of Pride at Work, the AFL-CIO group for lesbian, gay, bisexual, and transgender members.

To kick things off, the fledging group advertised a public forum for LGBT workers. But the event was a failure—speakers outnumbered attendees.

Watts realized that outreach would have to be more personal, and that the group would have to make people feel safe. Few LGBT workers in the area were "out" on the job.

So she began personally approaching LGBT workers from different unions to ask if they would help form a chapter. That worked better.

"We focused on creating relationships," Watts says, "rather than fixating on growing membership numbers."

She also quickly realized that "you can't expect people to support your cause if you don't support theirs." So to build relationships, Pride at Work members walked picket lines, made signs, worked phonebanks, and canvassed for any union who needed help.

"My wife claims I drank beer with blue-collar union guys for two years before asking for their support for same-sex marriage equality," Watts says.

It worked. When the legislature began discussing marriage equality in New York state, almost every union in Rochester—including the police and firefighters—actively pushed for the bill.

In fact, Rochester unions were instrumental in moving the Republican-controlled Senate to vote yes. A local Republican senator, who had voted against equality in the past, became the first to break ranks with his party and support it.

"I could not have been prouder of my union sisters and brothers," Watts says. "Now Pride at Work is an integrated part of the Rochester labor community. We pulled LGBT workplace concerns out of the closet by creating visibility and building relationships."

'We focused on creating relationships.'

#8

YOU GOTTA LOOK THEM IN THE EYE

Slobodan Dmitrov

Email, texting, leaflets, Facebook, and websites are great—but as Bess Watts found out, they can't take the place of one-on-one conversations. Talking face to face is still the best way to get people involved and convince them to take action.

It's easy to read a leaflet and then toss it. But when a real person is asking you, it's harder to say no.

Remember from Lesson 1 that you have to diagnose the obstacles to organizing. What looks like apathy might really be fear, hopelessness, confusion, or division. A flyer can't figure out what's holding people back, nor can it help them to get over it. For that you need two-way communication. You have to talk with your co-workers—and more important, listen to them.

Where can these conversations happen? In the break room, the cafeteria, the parking lot, or even while you're working (if that's feasible at your job).

But many organizers have found that a more relaxed and honest conversation is possible when you're both off the clock, and not someplace where "the walls have ears." If you have a chance to grab a coffee or a beer with your co-workers, or join their carpool, take it! You'll find out things you never knew.

> When a real person is asking you, it's harder to say no.

#9 TWO EARS, ONE MOUTH

Organizing involves a lot more listening than talking. Try the 80/20 rule—listen 80 percent of the time, talk 20 percent. Or at least get your share down to a third: you have two ears and one mouth, so use them proportionately.

This can be hard, especially when you're excited, or when you have information that others lack. But listening is crucial if you're going to find out what makes someone tick.

Consider your own experience. How does it feel to be talked at by someone who only seems interested in the sound of her own voice? Or when a friend is so wrapped up in his own concerns that you can't get a word in edgewise?

When you got a chance to say what was on your mind, weren't you a lot more invested in the conversation and whatever came after it?

When your co-workers tell you what they care about, remember it.

"You have to listen," says Maria Martínez, who was the chief steward in the meatpacking plant you read about in Lesson 1, where members organized against harassment. "It's really important to let people let out their feelings and for them to see that someone cares about what they have to say.

UFCW Local 4CO (CC BY 2.0) bit.ly/1oNT5dN

"Then you can ask them, 'What do you think we should do about it?' You can say, 'I think we should do this.' But I've learned it's more effective when the ideas come out of them."

To get the other person talking, ask open-ended questions. For example: "What would you like to see in the next contract?" Don't assume you already know the answer. Avoid questions that will probably get you a simple yes or no, such as: "Would you like a raise in the next contract?"

When your co-workers tell you what they care about, remember it. Later on, when you're asking them to take some kind of action, your success will depend on showing how that action relates to the issues that matter to them.

HOW TO BE A GOOD LISTENER

- **Avoid distractions.** Look the other person in the eye, and put your phone away.

- **Slow down.** Our brains process thoughts four times faster than spoken words. It's easy to skip ahead in a conversation, using your assumptions to fill in the gaps and plan your response. Resist this urge. Focus on what is actually being said.

- **Don't interrupt.** Take the time to hear the full story.

- **Keep an open mind.** Don't assume you already know what someone cares about. People will surprise you.

- **Don't fish.** Avoid leading questions like "Don't you agree that..."

- **Practice empathy.** Sometimes people need to let off steam. Don't discourage them. Your immediate task is to hear what they have to say, not to judge.

- **Show that you hear what they're saying.** React, ask follow-up questions, and repeat back what you understood. If you don't understand, ask.

- **Find common ground.** You don't have to agree with every point, but look for areas of agreement, and acknowledge where you differ.

- **Don't feel you need to sell something.** An organizer is not a salesperson. You're genuinely looking to learn the other person's point of view and create something new together.

Adapted from "Effective Listening" by David Kameras, *Steward Update Newsletter,* Union Communication Services

Download this at *labornotes.org/ secrets*

#10

IT ALL STARTS WITH RESPECT

Bernard Pollack (CC BY 2.0) *bit.ly/1oXfGFk*

When the relationships are tight, everyone feels safer and it's easier to take risks.

When you have self-respect, it means you won't put up with bullying or exploitation. When you respect your co-workers, it means you value their experience and know they have something important to add to the plan for solving problems at work.

You can just declare respect. It's built by forming personal relationships, the kind where you have each other's backs—like Bess Watts did by getting to know those "blue-collar union guys" in Rochester, drinking beer together and walking their picket lines. That doesn't happen overnight.

Why do we have to make it personal? Because organizing is scary for most people, at times even ourselves. No one wants to get in trouble for rocking the boat. The most effective way to address that fear is to link people together. When the relationships are tight, everyone feels safer and it's easier to take risks. Superficial connections won't withstand management's pressure tactics.

Kay Eisenhower was a "founding mother" of a Service Employees local in Alameda County, California. She recalls, "One of my favorite examples from the hospital was when the clerks got together to create a break space out of a deserted nurses station. We cleaned out the refuse, brought plants and kitchen stuff from home—we carved out our own little space."

It was a space where connections were reinforced every day, and more important because the clerks had made it themselves.

IN-DEPTH CONVERSATIONS

When new leaders took over the Chicago Teachers Union in 2010, they inherited a tradition of phonebanking for political candidates. But they turned phonebanking into a way to have in-depth conversations with members.

"The heart of our trainings," said organizer Matthew Luskin, "was to keep people from treating these like calls to get someone out to an event. Instead it was about learning members' concerns, along with discussing the strategy to win.

"We wanted to make sure that younger members were in dialogue with the union activists, that we were listening to what issues were important to them, what they were willing to fight for, what fears they had."

New members were often the least involved with the union, and the most scared to take action. So in the year before the union's contract expired, phonebanks focused on calling members with three years or less.

Special education teacher Margo Murray says the union's organizing department trained her to describe the school board's goals, listen to members' thoughts, and project a vision of how the union could win.

Members were asked to do something—come to a rally, attend a training, join their school's contract committee or parent outreach, or fill buses to the state capital. Callers also advised members to save money in their personal "strike funds," in case of a strike.

"At first the response was, 'I'm not going on strike, I have all these student loans, I can't afford to spend any time out of work,'" Murray said. "I would say, 'Can you afford to spend time *in* work if they end up destroying our contract?'

"I talked about the things they wanted to take away from us, and one of the biggest things was lanes and steps [which gave higher pay for more education and seniority]. I said, 'If they take that away, you'll get no credit in your pay for getting that expensive degree.'

"I went into the history: what happens when unions have to go up against management and we end up being divided instead of united," she said. "The conversation usually lasted 20 or 30 minutes. By that time they were extremely receptive."

Ronnie Reese, CTU

#11
PEOPLE MOVE LITTLE BY LITTLE

Remember the bullseye chart from Lesson 1. You're not trying to move someone from disengaged to organizer in one conversation, but maybe from disengaged to supportive, or from supportive to active, or from active to part of the core group. Slow and steady wins the race.

There's one major exception to this rule. When people are in a high-stakes fight where they're forced into action against a powerful enemy, it can change their thinking overnight. But most times, you will make better progress, and be less prone to disappointment, if you expect people to dip their toes in gradually.

Don't give up on people because of one "no." They may warm up over time. There may be things they're willing to do that neither of you has thought of yet.

CWA Local 2108

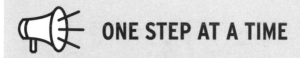

ONE STEP AT A TIME

Organizer Paul Krehbiel remembers talking to a medical technologist at Los Angeles County Hospital, who complained that the union didn't do much. Krehbiel asked him to sign a petition about a workplace problem.

"What's the point?" the guy asked. "It won't do any good."

Krehbiel explained that the petition alone wasn't expected to fix the problem, but it was part of a long-term campaign. If the petition didn't get results, the stewards were planning to attach it to a group grievance. Next they would get as many people as possible to attend the grievance meeting and speak out. The technologist signed the petition.

Sure enough, even after 70 percent of the workers signed, management refused to fix the problem. So the union filed a group grievance.

The next time Krehbiel saw him, the medical technologist was more interested. He asked if the grievance meeting had been set yet, and he brought up a complaint he and some others had on another issue. Just a little bit of participation had begun to change his perspective.

#12

GET SPECIFIC

Choose a manageable task, at least to start off.

Ask your co-workers to take a specific action. Choose a manageable task. Don't make it seem like an open-ended commitment. Be clear about how much time it will take, why you're doing it, and how it fits into the overall plan.

Here's an unproductive approach: "A few of us are carrying the whole burden and doing everything in the union. We really need you to get involved." (This request has the added disadvantage of being a guilt trip.)

AFL-CIO

What's a better way? "We're trying to reach 200 people about the dangerous temperatures in the plant lately. Can you be a part of the phonebank next Tuesday or Wednesday night?" This request defines the task (make calls), the time (Tuesday or Wednesday night), the goal (reach 200 people), and the issue (dangerous temperatures).

If this co-worker had never phonebanked before, you could improve the request further by explaining what to expect. "A few of us will sit together for two hours and call our co-workers. You'll have a list of phone numbers and a loose script to help you along, including three questions we're asking everybody. Afterwards we'll tally the answers and discuss what we learned."

MAKE SIGNS FROM SCRATCH

If you're planning a picket, hold a sign-making party ahead of time. A party will bring members together, let them discuss the boss's latest outrage, and encourage them to show their creativity. The sign-makers will be proud of their signs and will show up to picket.

RED-SHIRT FRIDAYS

Chicago Teachers Union

As the Chicago teachers built up to their 2012 strike, one tactic they used to get people warmed up for bigger actions—and to keep track of their growing support—was asking members to wear red every Friday.

The genius of "wear red" is its simplicity. It's something concrete and low-risk that a steward can ask anyone to do, even someone who has no extra time.

At first, many members would just wear a red scarf or a red-patterned blouse on Fridays. But the visibility helped to calm fears. Co-workers who were on the fence could see for themselves the growing level of union support as red spread throughout their school.

The weekly action also gave stewards a reason to talk regularly with their co-workers. Any excuse for a conversation is another organizing opportunity.

Charlotte Sanders was a steward working to organize her fellow paraprofessionals, scattered across many different schools. "On Thursday I would send a text and say, 'Tomorrow is spirit day,'" she said. "I made personal phone calls, which was good because I could touch base about how their week went."

As excitement and confidence grew, more and more people ordered red union T-shirts. The union started selling them at its monthly delegates' meetings. "People would come in with orders for their whole school," recalled Debby Pope, a grievance rep.

Administrators noticed. Students noticed. Members loved it. Many sent in group photos from their schools, all in red, for the union website. At the height of the campaign, nine out of 10 schools had members wearing red on Fridays in big numbers.

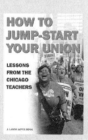

When the strike came, Sanders told her co-workers, "This is going to be your red badge of courage." Red T-shirts became the strike uniform, and community members recognized what they stood for.

Read more in *How to Jump-Start Your Union.*

 # AN ORGANIZING CONVERSATION

Here are some guidelines for a fruitful conversation (or a series of conversations) with a co-worker.

Nobody should follow a script mechanically, of course. Talk with people like human beings! But think of this outline as a tool. The steps can help you move toward a goal, so your co-worker isn't left feeling like her time's been wasted with a spiel or a gripe session. Done right, an organizing conversation leads to action.

Your job is mostly to ask questions. You want your co-worker to realize:

- She cares about a problem.
- There's a decision-maker who has the power to fix this problem.
- The decision-maker won't fix it until someone pushes them to.
- If your co-worker really wants this problem fixed, she has to join you and other co-workers in taking action.

But just telling her all this wouldn't be very effective. Instead, you want to ask the right questions that get her to say it herself. We tend to remember what we said, not what the other person said.

1. DISCOVER THE ISSUES

Begin by asking questions—and listening to the answers—to learn what your co-worker cares about. Make your questions open-ended, especially when you're getting to know someone.

> *How's your day going?*

> *How did you get this job?*

> *What was it like when you first started here?*

When you're organizing around a particular issue, your questions might get more pointed. Still, even if you have a petition about the awful new schedule, don't leap straight into "Will you sign this?" Instead, ask:

> *How's the new schedule working for you?*

The point is for your co-worker to remind herself how she feels about this problem, before you ask her to act. If you've discussed this issue before, you can still ask how it's affecting her today, or share someone else's story and get her reaction.

2. AGITATE

React to what she tells you, and ask follow-up questions. By reacting, the organizer can help the other person feel she has permission to be angry:

Wow. How long has that been going on?

How does that make you feel?

Is that okay with you?

How are you coping?

How is that affecting your family?

3. LAY THE BLAME

Get her talking about who's responsible.

Why do you think we're having this problem?

Who's in a position to fix it? What would they have to do?

Do you think this problem is going to correct itself?

Many times we feel our problems are just "the way things are." Realizing that bad conditions didn't fall from the sky can be empowering. If someone made the decision that caused this mess, that someone could also unmake it.

4. MAKE A PLAN TO WIN

Now that your co-worker is angry, it's time to offer some hope. Hope comes from your power in numbers and a winnable plan. That's how you make your problem into a problem for the decision-maker.

> *Most people want to go back to the old schedule. The supervisor hasn't listened, but what if 25 of us sign this petition, and we all march into his office together to deliver it?*

> *What do you think he'll do? Will he be able to keep ignoring us?*

> *What's his boss going to say?*

This step will be trickier if today's petition doesn't address a problem that this person feels strongly about. You'll have an easier time organizing if you choose issues that are widely and deeply felt—we'll talk about that in Lesson 4.

But what you can say is that power in numbers is our only way to get a say on any issue. For instance:

> *If we win on this issue, do you think management will learn something? Will taking action on the next issue be easier?*

> *This is the first step. We've all got to start backing each other up. How else are we going to build enough power to fix the understaffing you're talking about?*

5. GET A COMMITMENT

Ask the member to be part of the solution by taking a specific action.

> *Will you sign this petition and come with us to deliver it on Thursday?*

If someone is fearful, acknowledge that her fears have real reasons behind them. But still, things won't get better unless she gets involved. Your job isn't to convince her that she's wrong about her fears, but that she needs to act anyway.

> *Is the schedule ever going to get fixed if we don't take action? Are you willing to let this problem go on?*

Helping her through it will be a lot easier when you're inviting her to act on what she's already said— not pushing an action you're trying to "sell."

6. INOCULATE AND RE-COMMIT

Now your co-worker is committed—but does she know what she's getting into? Ask how she thinks management will react to the action.

> *What do you think the supervisor will say when we go to his office?*

If there's a likely risk she hasn't thought of, warn her about it.

> *What if he gets angry and threatens to write everyone up? What if he offers to meet with one or two of us but not the whole group?*

Talk through the possible outcomes. Then ask whether you can still count on her participation.

> *Does any of that change your mind?*

This part might sound like you're undermining your organizing. You've gone to all this work to help your co-worker decide to act, and now you're trying to talk her out of it? But like inoculating against a virus, the idea is to help her develop an immunity to management's attacks—by giving her a small dose before she's exposed to the real thing.

This way, when management reacts, she won't be thrown by it. In fact, your correct prediction will boost your credibility.

7. SET A FOLLOW-UP PLAN

As organizer Fred Ross put it, "90 percent of organizing is follow-up."

Agree on the next step, and when you'll check back in. Maybe she's going to meet you Thursday to deliver the petition, or she'll ask two co-workers to sign. Or maybe you simply promise to report back on Friday about how the meeting went.

Remember, you're not just trying to pull off this one action. You're also trying to draw people gradually closer to the center and build an ongoing network of communication. You're trying to make standing up, in an organized way, a normal and natural part of workplace life.

> *Can you ask Jane to sign? Great! I'll come back at the end of the shift to find out how it went, okay?*

A.H.U.Y. THERE!

The acronym "A.H.U.Y." is a helpful shorthand for what it takes to move someone to act:

Anger: This is an injustice. We have to fix this.

Hope: Change is possible. We can fix this. Here's our plan.

Urgency: Now's the time. We can't wait any longer.

You can make a difference. Your participation matters.

EXERCISE:
WRITE YOUR OWN ORGANIZING CONVERSATION

Choose a real **issue** from your own workplace and a possible **action** you might organize to address it. Choose a real **co-worker** and imagine you're going to approach him or her about joining you in action.

You want to cover all the bases of a good organizing conversation. What questions would you ask at each step?

1. Discover the issues.

2. Agitate.

3. Lay the blame.

4. Make a plan to win.

5. Get a commitment.

6. Inoculate and re-commit.

7. Set a follow-up plan.

Download this at
labornotes.org/secrets

EXERCISE:
PRACTICE THE ORGANIZING
CONVERSATION OUT LOUD

It can feel awkward at first, encouraging your co-workers to get mad and challenging them to face their fears. But like anything, it gets easier with practice.

If you're reading this in a workshop or as a group, pair up and practice the conversation. Take turns playing the role of organizer. If you're reading this on your own, ask an experienced organizer to be your partner, or recruit a friend or family member to try it out.

Ask about the other person's real job, whatever it is. Pretend you work there too, but you don't know much yet—maybe you're new. Have him give you a plausible setting for the conversation, such as the lunchroom. Ask him to do his best to answer your questions honestly, as if this were for real.

Start with *issues*. Ask as many questions as you can think of, to find out what he loves and hates about the work, what's changed over time, what he would fix if he had a magic wand. Don't rush.

When you think you've zeroed in on the issue he cares about most, move into *agitation* and *laying the blame*. See if you can get him to say out loud that he's ready to do something to solve this problem, and to name who's responsible.

Move into a *plan to win*, and inspire him with the idea of strength in numbers. Ask him to *commit* to a specific action. Do some *inoculation* about the risks and ask him to recommit. Set a *follow-up plan*, when you will be back in touch.

Afterwards, debrief with your partner. Find out how he felt about the conversation.

Did you correctly identify his top-priority issue? What else could you have asked about? What parts of the conversation really made him think? What parts did he enjoy?

If he agreed to take the action, why did he decide to do it? If he didn't, what could have made him reconsider?

Download this at
labornotes.org/secrets

These one-on-one conversations will be the building blocks of your organizing. But you probably can't have in-depth talks with every person in your workplace—there are only 24 hours in a day! Plus, you've probably found some co-workers you can't get through to. For you, they're like a brick wall. Someone else might have better luck, if only you had a team working in sync.

So how do you figure out who to start with? Which people do you want to draw into the core group? How can you form a communication network that reaches everybody? Find out in **Lesson 3: Map Your Workplace and Its Leaders.**

LESSON 3:
MAP YOUR
WORKPLACE
AND ITS LEADERS

You've learned the art of one-on-one conversations. You've recognized that you don't need to recruit everyone at once, and gotten past the assumption that "nobody cares." Organizing starts with the resources you have. Maybe for now it's just you and one other person.

Next you'll want to analyze the power and relationships that exist in your workplace already. One of the smartest ways to start is by drawing up a comprehensive picture of your workplace. Understanding who does what where—including in management—is your first step to shifting power.

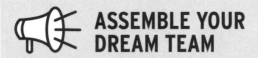

ASSEMBLE YOUR DREAM TEAM

At a Chicago hospital Emergency Department, stewards had tried petitioning management to address dangerous understaffing, but to no avail. To increase the pressure, they decided to organize a boycott of overtime.

"We got out the map of the entire department," said steward Dennis Kosuth, "all different shifts, the observation area, the pediatric area. We had to make sure to have people in those areas on all shifts.

"We knew which people had pull among the different cliques or groups at work. I went to those people first, and they would spread the word to other people.

'I went to the people with pull first and they would spread the word.'

"I was looking for the people who say what they think, even if I don't always agree with them. The people who are seen by their co-workers, and even by management sometimes, as leaders in the workplace. Not the person who goes to management because 'this person looked at me funny' but those who will say to their supervisors, 'We need to have more help here,' or go to their co-workers and say, 'This isn't safe.'"

Among 130 nurses and dozens of paramedics, there were many immigrants and more than a dozen ethnic groups: Filipino, Indian, Nigerian, Eritrean, Mexican, Puerto Rican, white, African American, Thai, Chinese, Haitian, Liberian, Polish, and Jamaican.

"At the start of organizing the overtime boycott," said Kosuth, "I heard things like, 'The Nigerians are each supporting 10 families back home, they need the money too much to go along.' Or some of my co-workers would tell me, 'The nurses from India are made to work overtime by their husbands, and they won't go against them.'

"I said, 'Let's go ask them.' I would bring them with me and they could hear the Indian nurses' reaction for themselves: 'We don't think a one-day boycott is enough. We think it should be two weeks.'"

The stewards used their workplace map another way, too. They wanted managers to know an overtime boycott was being planned, but they didn't want to inform the boss themselves. So they took note of which nurses would be likely to carry the news to management—and made sure those nurses were informed.

The boycott succeeded beyond anyone's expectations. Management agreed to hire more staff. Afterward, Kosuth said, "the sentiment was, 'No matter where we come from, when we stick together, nobody can stop us.'"

#13 PEOPLE ARE ALREADY ORGANIZED

Jim West, jimwestphoto.com

Your next task is to find and build on the organization that's already there.

Your workplace may feel like a disorganized mess. But the truth is, you're not starting from zero. There's organization there already—though it might not have anything to do with the union.

Are there carpools, for instance? Family ties? A rumor mill?

If John didn't show up for his shift, who would have his number and call him up to find out if he was okay? If Monique came out of the supervisor's office in tears, who would meet her in the break room to give her a hug and ask what happened?

People are social creatures who form bonds anywhere we go. But it's especially true in a workplace, where we're under pressure and relying on each other to get things done. We get to know each other's strengths and weaknesses, and size up who we can trust. We figure out ways to pass around important news.

So your next task is to find and build on the organization that's already there. First you'll need to map out the many existing networks, and then you'll begin to knit them together into your union network.

#14 TAP INTO EXISTING GROUPS

Erik McGregor

Every workplace is organized at least two ways—the way management has designed things and the way workers themselves organize. You should understand both.

There are **work groups** created by management, people who interact every day because of the work they do. For instance, the Emergency Department described above was divided into various work spaces (the observation area, the pediatric area), jobs (nurses, paramedics), and shifts.

Different work groups will have different degrees of power on the job, depending on factors such as skill and whether they're in a position to bottleneck the flow of work. Certain jobs are ideally positioned to be nodes of communication—for instance, in a hospital, the cafeteria cashiers and the transporters who wheel patients around.

Both work groups and social groups create connections among their members.

There are also **social groups**, who may hang out at lunchtime or outside of work. Who buys lottery tickets together? Who shares a running joke? Social groups often form among people who have something in common—for instance, smokers, young workers, people who attend the same church, or people who speak the same language.

Both work groups and social groups create connections among their members. You can draw on these connections to figure out strategies that unite your co-workers, and use people's natural tendency to stick up for those close to them.

BRINGING THE WORK GROUPS TOGETHER

At an auto parts factory where transmission cases were die-casted, the two main work groups were machine operators and inspectors. Management didn't allow inspectors to talk to operators.

At one point management increased the production quotas. The speed-up immediately put pressure on the operators making the pieces. But soon the inspectors too were having trouble keeping up, causing them to mark many of the pieces as scrap. Under stress, operators and inspectors tended to blame each other.

Eventually the leaders of the two groups got together and worked out an arrangement: the inspectors would mark as scrap any case with the tiniest flaw, causing the scrap to pile up.

Jim West, jimwestphoto.com

Management would have to turn off the machines to find the problems.

Soon each machine was experiencing several hours of downtime every day. After a week of this, management reduced the quota.

Another time, an operator was fired on trumped-up charges. The leader of that group asked key skilled tradespeople, who had easy access to everyone in the plant, to spread the word that something was going to happen in the lunchroom.

Organizers asked the key people to make sure everyone participated.

At lunch break, workers discussed the situation and decided on a symbolic action. The next day black armbands were handed out in the parking lot.

Organizers asked the key people in each group to make sure the action had broad participation. They suggested that everyone has an "off" day sometimes, when things just don't seem to go right—and it would be a shame if everyone had an off day at the same time.

After two days of this, the machine operator was brought back to work. Such an action would have been impossible if the shop floor organizers hadn't recognized the work groups and the social groups, and the leaders in each.

#15
BEWARE OF DIVIDE AND CONQUER

Dan Lutz

Nurses overcame the stereotype that the union is only for certain people.

Often social groups will form along racial or ethnic lines. Sometimes even work groups are racially segregated, because of management's hiring or promotion policies. In these cases, you need to be doubly sensitive and make sure that from the start you're involving leaders from all groups.

Think about the overtime boycott described at the beginning of this lesson. The boycott relied on strength in numbers—it wouldn't have succeeded if only one or two ethnic groups had participated. Organizers took a deliberate approach to overcoming their co-workers' prejudices.

Another hospital example: When Judy Sheridan-Gonzalez, now president of the New York State Nurses, first started working at Montefiore Medical Center, people told her not to bother trying to engage the Asian nurses—they wouldn't be interested in the union.

But an issue soon came to light that hit Filipinas hardest. Nurses on H-1 guestworker visas were being threatened that they would lose their visas if they got involved with the union. Some were forced to endure inferior living conditions, including "hot beds," where a day-shift nurse and a night-shift nurse shared a bed on a rotating schedule.

Gonzalez pushed for the union to offer legal advice—which got an overwhelming response from the Filipina nurses. And learning about the exploitative conditions unified nurses of all backgrounds. Soon a similar situation emerged, affecting Jamaican nurses.

Filipina and Jamaican nurses together led the campaign to put a stop to these practices. Nurses from other ethnicities joined in. After they won, word spread to other hospitals, ultimately ending these practices throughout the region.

Though that was decades ago, Gonzalez says, nurses from many countries continue to count themselves as union activists at Montefiore. It's one of the union's strongest hospitals, in part because workers overcame the stereotype that the union is only for certain people.

UNION TIME, *TIEMPO DEL SINDICATO*

Jim West, jimwestphoto.com

When workers were organizing a union at the Smithfield hog processing plant in Tarheel, North Carolina, there was not much contact between Latino workers, who were the majority, and African American workers, who made up most of the rest of the workforce. Few Latino immigrants spoke much English, and the African American workers spoke no Spanish.

In the course of the campaign, a movement grew on the shop floor for workers to write "Union Time" on their work helmets. Management reacted. A Latino worker was called into the office and threatened with discipline.

As he came out of the office, looking bummed, an African American union supporter saw him.

Somehow, they managed a conversation. The Latino worker got across that he was about to get in trouble.

So the black worker took his own helmet and wrote on it *"Tiempo del Sindicato"*—"Union Time" in Spanish. He handed it to the Latino worker to wear, and put the "Union Time" helmet on his own head. They high-fived.

News moves quickly through a plant. When the incident came up at the next union meeting, everyone cheered.

At one point up to a thousand workers were wearing "Union Time" or *"Tiempo del Sindicato"* on their helmets. The union filed an unfair labor practice charge, and eventually the company issued a written apology in English and Spanish for suppressing union talk.

Acting together across the language barrier helped propel the workers to winning their union.

Enforcing this important right, and acting together across the language barrier, helped propel the workers to winning their union.

#16 LOOK FOR NATURAL LEADERS

Somos un Pueblo Unido

Every workplace has informal leaders who aren't elected or appointed; they just *are*, and they influence others in their group. If you have a message to communicate, reach the leaders of the informal groups. You can bet the word will get out to everyone.

Think about your co-workers, and ask around. When someone has a problem, who do they go to for help, defense, or advice? Who do they ask when they want the facts? Who do they trust, respect, admire? Certain names usually come up over and over. In one hospital, a certain nurse was known on his floor as "the mayor."

Don't just ask—watch. Organizer Ellen Norton suggested that you observe carefully when people are together. "We look for workers who can answer co-workers' questions," she said. "We observe the dynamics in the room. Who responds? Who defers to whom? Who understands the union? Who understands what the boss is doing? Is everyone mentioning a worker who is not present? I want to meet that person.

"We also look for people who are good judges of their co-workers. How well did they describe their co-workers' interests and concerns before they brought them to the meeting?"

When management goes on the offensive, who responds in a way that educates her co-workers? Who is able to soothe their fears afterward?

Fundamentally, a *leader* is someone who has *followers*. That means there are others who will take an action—sign the petition, wear the sticker, attend the rally, join the strike—when this person asks.

There are usually multiple leaders in a workplace, often tied to the many work and social groups. Different leaders might have sway among the younger workers, the moms, the basketball players, the people who work in a certain department, or the night shift. There might be leaders of different social cliques. Someone might have just one or two followers.

What if you're not the leader? You probably aren't—at least, not for everyone. Maybe your friend Ann follows your lead, but you sense that Ben doesn't trust you. You've noticed he always waits to see what Carlos is going to do.

That doesn't make you a failure. On the contrary, you're thinking like an organizer. You've spotted another possible leader, Carlos.

FINDING LEADERS IN A MEATPACKING PLANT

In Lesson 1 you read how stewards in a meatpacking plant in Pasco, Washington, organized their co-workers to resist harassment. But to do that, the core group of activists first had to find and recruit the natural leaders.

Maria Chávez was at the meeting where potential leaders were discussed. "We drew a map of the plant and made a list of all the production lines," she said. "We sat down by lines to choose 'volunteers.' The job of the volunteers was to inform people on their line, to distribute flyers, invite them to meetings, and answer their questions."

"Our goal was to have three 'volunteers' on each line," said her co-worker, Maria Martínez. (A line could have 20 to 40 workers.) "We looked for people who didn't let management push them around, and for people who had a good way of expressing themselves and speaking out.

"That didn't mean we were looking for the loudest or pushiest people. Some of the best leaders had a really quiet way about them. We looked for people that management respected and that workers respected."

Martínez also looked for people who weren't disciplined often. "When you see a person like that speaking up," she said, "you think there must be a real problem going on here. Also, it was harder for management to retaliate against members who were known as hard workers with good records."

'We looked for people that management respected and that workers respected.'

Once they had their list of potential recruits, Martínez, Chávez, and the other planners divided up the list and began holding organizing conversations like the ones described in Lesson 2. They sat down with each one in the cafeteria and asked how she felt about work, giving her a chance to express her frustrations.

"I'd explain what we were doing," Martínez said. "that we were building a network to get people together to try to make changes." She would invite the person to a meeting of other volunteers.

"That's when we started to lose our fear," said Chávez. At the meetings, "we saw that we weren't alone. And we had a plan for working together to achieve something."

BRING THE LEADERS TOGETHER AS A TEAM

Remember the bullseye model from Lesson 1. The people who already have followers are the ones you want to draw into your core group of organizers and the next circle of activists. These are the people you should spend the most time with.

The people who already have followers are the ones to draw into your core group.

Go out of your way to get to know them. Have good organizing conversations where you mostly listen, learn what they care about, and help them develop the organizing attitude. Time spent with these leaders will pay dividends.

As your organizing continues, you will always be on the lookout for new leaders. In a union drive, Norton said, "we constantly build the organizing committee throughout the campaign. We might give one committee member unsigned union cards, but another co-worker brings the signed cards back. That's a potential committee member. Who gets their co-workers to wear buttons, come out to leaflet, or march on the boss? They are committee members."

Most people are both leaders and followers. The union president might look to one rank and filer to be his tech guru and another to navigate city politics. Someone might be the acknowledged leader of her work group but always follow the lead of the chief steward.

Each individual leader doesn't need to know how to do everything—but a team of leaders, together, can combine the qualities that will make your campaigns succeed.

The strength of any core group will depend on how many people look to its members for leadership. If there are holes in your core group, there will be holes in your participation. For instance, if no respected leader from the night shift is involved, don't be surprised when you can't get many night shifters to join the sticker day.

THE ONE-TO-TEN RULE

A strong organizing team should include leaders from every department and shift, and from every social group. Aim for one core-group organizer or activist for every 10 workers.

For instance, in a department of 30 workers, you want three activists—ideally not just any three people, but the three most influential leaders, representing different work or social groups.

LEADER VS. LEADER

Dan Lutz

On one hospital unit, organizer Marsha Niemeijer recalled "a classic divide. Everyone is angry at the horrible manager, but the high-seniority nurses have found ways to manage it. The low-seniority nurses bear the brunt of the manager's abuse, so they want to do something."

Tensions flared up when a nurse filed a complaint against five co-workers. Two leaders among the less-senior nurses wrote up a petition defending them.

Niemeijer coached the young women by phone on how to begin gathering signatures. "I worked with them because they were responsive, fast, and anxious to do something," she said, "all good reasons, but not enough." The missing ingredient was buy-in from senior nurse leaders.

The first day went well. But after the petition was handed off to the night shift, a senior nurse took it, refused to sign it, and held it all night so he could talk it over with another nurse who was considered the day-shift leader. The two men were frustrated that they hadn't been consulted first.

"They thought we should have met first as a unit and come up with a plan of action," Niemeijer said. "They were right."

On the other hand, "one of the female nurses who started the petition was upset, and she was also right, that even though the day-shift leader should have been consulted, he could have respected the initiative and asked to consult or regroup, instead of killing the whole thing."

The snafu reflected the divisions between more- and less-senior nurses—and perhaps between men and women, too. The young nurses discovered that some of their co-workers would follow their lead, but others wouldn't.

"We had different leadership structures in this one unit," Niemeijer concluded, "and hadn't done enough to bring them all together." As a result, "we lost momentum, and that organizing opportunity died down. But we debriefed, we learned, and those leaders are back up and running with new skills."

The missing ingredient was buy-in from senior leaders.

#18

IT'S NOT THE LOUDEST PERSON

AFSCME Council 31

LaKesha Harrison helped form Member Action Teams (MATs) in her AFSCME local. She warned, "The person who jumps up and says 'I'm the leader' is usually not the real leader. They just want to be the union person, the person with the information, the one who saves the day.

> **Leadership is not about doing things for other people.**

"But leadership is not about doing things for other people. It's about getting them to do things for themselves."

Nor is the chronic complainer necessarily your best ally. The person who's known as a whiner is unlikely to have co-workers' respect.

Some people will volunteer as leaders but they can't follow through. They can't bring others around. They're too cautious, or they're not really liked by their co-workers. If that becomes apparent, you could ask that person to introduce you to other potential leaders in the department.

To separate the posers from the true leaders, Harrison used little tests. "We ask a potential MAT leader to bring four people to a meeting or get a bunch of flyers out," Harrison said. "They do these things and they become the MAT organizer.

"Often, they've done this stuff already. They're already trying to be helpful, because they're natural leaders."

#19
EVERYONE HAS ROOM TO GROW

Alexandra Bradbury

As important as it is to seek out those with natural leadership qualities, you'll find they still have plenty of room to grow.

Some might have big egos, struggle to control their tempers, or even be shy. Some might be in the habit of doing all the union work themselves, instead of involving their co-workers.

As an organizer, part of your job is to help leaders in your workplace develop their skills and become stronger leaders.

"Leaders often emerge from fights, even failed ones," Niemeijer says. "And how you support them, how you let them lead during that fight, what you talk through with them during the fight, how you debrief with them after the fight, is what it is all about. A leader who goes through a fight comes out of that with more depth, sophistication, and skills."

Nurses in one hospital department had just finished a campaign that got lots of people involved, battling understaffing. To keep the organizing going, the two main leaders decided to start an elected union committee for the department. To their surprise, lots of people wanted to join. Fifteen ran and 12 were elected.

Niemeijer talked with the two primary leaders about the bullseye model. She encouraged them to think about which of the new committee members already showed leadership qualities. "You two don't have the capacity to develop all 12 at the same time," she told them.

"You should assess who are the two or three who are most likely to move into the center of the bullseye with you. Those are the ones you want to encourage to become more like you. When there are four or five of you, then those four or five can work on the others."

Your job is to help leaders develop their skills and become stronger leaders.

HELP LEADERS LEARN

Here are a few ways activists can help each other develop as leaders:

- **Agree on your goals.** Your bottom line is to build the power of union members. Talk about it and come to an agreement on what building that power means in your workplace and beyond. (You'd be surprised how many leaders are not clear that power comes from active members.)

- **Hold each other accountable.** When you take an organizing assignment like talking to so-and-so, follow through on it, and make clear you expect the same from other leaders.

- **Team up.** Stay in frequent touch, and help each other problem-solve. Leaders with complementary skills can cross-train each other. Niemeijer says, "I had a leader who had great people skills, but she was nervous to 'round' [walk through the whole workplace checking in with everyone] through the hospital, so she would round with me. I would model one-on-one organizing conversations, show her how to navigate management, where all the break rooms were, and how to constantly collect intel. I teamed her up with other leaders who round well. Now she's training others to round and we have raised expectations that rounding is part of a leader's responsibility."

- **Form trusting friendships.** Give extra weight to your relationships with leaders. Prioritize their texts and emails. If they're targeted, make sure you have their back.

- **Educate each other.** Pass around articles. Talk about the big picture.

Download this at *labornotes.org/ secrets*

#20
ORGANIZE DEMOCRATICALLY

We've put a lot of emphasis on the importance of leaders, but there's a flip side. Your co-workers might sign your petition out of personal loyalty or trust. But if your agenda isn't really theirs, there are limits to how much you can get people to do.

People can tell when they're in charge and when they're not.

When people go to the mat, it's because they care about what's at stake and feel like it's their fight. They're part of the team steering the ship. So organizing democratically isn't just the right thing to do; it's also the best way to build power.

Democracy has a structural side. For instance, are stewards elected or appointed? Is it hard for rank and filers to meet the qualifications to run for office? You can push to change these kinds of rules in your union's bylaws.

But democracy also goes deeper than what the bylaws say. It's about who's making the decisions, from the shop floor to union-wide activities. People can tell when they're in charge and when they're not. If you're going to ask people to take big risks, you'd better make sure they're part of the process to get there.

The rank-and-file reformers who were elected to lead the Chicago Teachers Union in 2010 took this principle to heart. Once they won office, they didn't tell everyone to go home and let them handle things. They pushed for more involvement, more debate, more discussion.

Sometimes that debate was rough-and-tumble. Sometimes it took a lot of time. A majority didn't necessarily agree yet with everything the new leaders were putting forth: risky tactics, untested strategies like parent alliances, and the need to build towards a strike.

But the leaders, who wanted to radically transform their union, recognized that they could only succeed if members owned the decisions. They argued for a clear vision and dove into democratic debate over the way forward—with faith that the members, when presented with the same facts and analysis the leaders had, would come to the same conclusions. They were right.

Unionism at its core is about taking action together. Too often, officers or staff present members with: "Here's the plan. Are you in, or are you out?" Sometimes this may be necessary, but it's not optimal—and it will limit how committed members are to the action.

Read more in *Democracy Is Power.*

It's much better to involve everyone in the process that leads you there. The choice to be "in or out" evaporates when everyone was "in" from the beginning.

DEMOCRACY MEANS EVERYONE

In a democratic union, every member should be able to participate—for instance, read the contract, attend meetings, and vote in elections—regardless of whether he has a disability or what language she speaks.

It might take organizing to push your local to add a wheelchair ramp, translate materials, or provide interpreters, but it's worth the effort. The union will be stronger when everyone can be involved.

After the Food and Commercial Workers began providing simultaneous interpretation between English and Spanish in meetings of its meatpacking division, "workers came up and said, 'I've been coming to these meetings for years, and this is the first time that I understood what was being said and what was going on,'" according to

Jim West, jimwestphoto.com

Belinda Thielen of the union's health and safety office.

The union will be stronger when everyone can be involved.

The best practice is to conduct meetings in both (or all) languages, so the non-English speakers aren't singled out. That's how they run workshops at Workers United, a union that represents retail and factory workers in New York and New Jersey. Some parts are in Spanish, others in English, and simultaneous interpretation goes both ways.

Service Employees Local 26 in Minnesota does the same thing, asking anyone who speaks only one language to wear an interpretation headset. Those who speak only English experience what it's like to have to use interpretation, too. This setup puts members on a more equal footing.

"Sometimes we think we'll just talk *at* people in their language, and that's good enough," says Thielen. "But every good trade unionist knows a huge part of our job is listening to people, trying to make sure it goes in both directions."

QUALITIES OF A GOOD ORGANIZER

- Effective organizers are **good at their jobs and respected** by the people they work with.

- They have the **trust of their co-workers.** Their opinions carry weight. When they offer advice, people listen.

- The best organizers are motivated by a **strong sense of justice** and clear principles.

- They're **responsible, honest, and compassionate.**

- They're confident, even **courageous.**

- Organizers must be **good listeners**. They know you don't have to be the most vocal to have the biggest impact.

- They **bring people together**, welcoming new co-workers on the job and looking for ways to involve every member.

- Organizers **move people to collective action.** They don't just solve problems alone—they equip their co-workers to solve problems together.

- They put the **interests of the group first**, ahead of their individual concerns.

- They don't operate as lone rangers. They **respect group decisions.**

- Good organizers are **knowledgeable about their contract**, but not afraid to admit when they don't know the answer.

- They can stay **cool under pressure** and handle stress and conflict.

- They're willing to **stand up to management**—and they can inspire others to stand up for themselves as well.

Adapted from the New York State Nurses Association

Download this at
*labornotes.org/
secrets*

#21

MAKE A MAP TO GUIDE YOU

Drawing a map will help you bring the work groups, social groups, and their leaders to light.

This visual tool will help you and your fellow organizers pool your knowledge to see who's where, who looks up to whom, who hangs out with whom, and who's facing the same problems. A map can help you set up a member-to-member network or identify where more stewards are needed. Most important, maps make power relationships visible.

Maps make power relationships visible.

Making the map should be a group effort. You'll find it useful at any stage of organizing—whether you're a longstanding committee in mid-campaign, or a group of would-be organizers just thinking about how to get started. Because it's visual, the map can aid communication even when not everyone speaks the same language. And it's fun!

CAN YOU GET A LIST?

It's best to work from a list of all employees in your workplace or department (whatever you're mapping). Otherwise it's surprisingly easy to forget people, especially those you don't work closely with, part-timers, or those with unique jobs.

Maybe you can get this list from your union office, especially if you're a steward. If not, is there a list at work you can discreetly copy or take a picture of? The boss may distribute an emergency phone list, or post a schedule. Be resourceful.

EXERCISE:
DRAW YOUR WORKPLACE MAP

You will need:
- Butcher paper
- Color markers
- Sticky dots

Start with the physical space. First, use a flipchart or large sheet of paper and a black marker to outline the area or building, showing entrances, exits, and windows. Label the offices, production lines, storage areas, shipping and receiving docks, lunchrooms, and bathrooms.

Add details such as machines, desks, and water coolers. If the building is large, make maps of different areas. Be sure the map is large enough to show the information clearly.

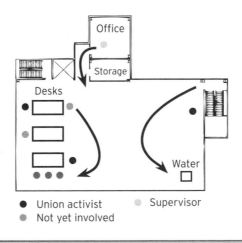

Add motion. Draw the flow of work or production, and/or the paths that different people take through the space regularly, in different colors.

Are there spots where the flow of work tends to get bottlenecked? These could be important pressure points. Who works there?

Are there places where people congregate, like the break room or the proverbial water cooler? These could be good places for outreach conversations, or group gatherings.

Add all the people. Sticky dots work well to represent workers. You might use different colors to indicate supervisors, union activists, various jobs, or shifts. Mark the dots with initials or names.

Download this at
labornotes.org/secrets

EXERCISE:
MAP OUT HOW PEOPLE CONNECT

Mark the groups. Draw a circle around the people who form each work group and each social group, using different colors. If members of a group are scattered all over, indicate them some other way, such as with a certain color or checkmark.

> Who works together?

> Who are all the smokers?

> Who carpools together?

> Who are the Spanish-speakers?

As you identify groups, discuss them.

> How does this group relate to management?

> What are the biggest problems affecting this group?

Keep your observations respectful and factual, not gossipy. The idea is to find insights that will help you organize with these co-workers, not repeat stereotypes or gripes about them.

Mark the leaders. Indicate each group's leader with a corresponding color.

> *Who's the main leader in this group?*

> *Are there other leaders in this group?*

Map out union support. Who's part of your organizing team so far? If there's not a formal group, choose some criteria.

> *Who gathered signatures on the latest petition?*

> *Who's helping to make this map?*

Also mark the wider circle of union supporters.

> *Who signed the last petition?*

> *Who is a dues-paying member?*

Download this at
labornotes.org/secrets

EXERCISE:
ANALYZE YOUR WORKPLACE MAP

Discuss your map. You now have a great deal of information about interactions in your workplace. This is a good place to stop and ask yourselves:

> *What do you see?*

Even when people know their workplace well, the map will help them see it with new eyes. Ask open-ended questions.

> *What's going on here?*

> *Do we see any patterns?*

> *How does news travel?*

> *What new questions does this map raise?*

The stories that come out will be about issues that are bothering people. Keep adding to the map, marking which workers are being harassed by management, for instance, and which are facing layoffs. If the map gets too crowded, start tracking the information another way.

Use your map to identify areas and leaders to focus on. Making workplace dynamics visible puts valuable information on the table.

> *See this group over here, the one we've never had contact with? Who can talk to someone in that group?*

The next time you go to work, look around and compare the reality to your map.

> *Did we overlook anyone?*

Download this at
labornotes.org/secrets

EXERCISE:
MAKE A CHART, TOO

In some workplaces, everyone moves all over the place, and a physical map would be a hopeless jumble. In that case, make a chart instead.

Even if you made a map, you'll find a chart helpful too. Charts are easy to update and allow you to see at a glance where your union is weak and where it's strong. Make a big version to display on the wall. Enter the same information into a spreadsheet you can print out and carry around with you.

Make a grid. You might use columns for different work areas or job titles, and rows for shifts.

Write in all the names. Some organizers include cell phone numbers and email addresses, to have all the info in one place.

Map the groups and leaders. As with the map, use colors and symbols to map out formal and in-formal connections. Discuss the same questions.

Color code the chart. Depending on your goals, you might highlight all the people who have committed to a rally, signed a petition, or worn a button.

Keep updating. Continually revise your chart. Track how people's union roles and relationships change.

SAMPLE CHART

	Dishwashers	**Room Service**
Day	Heather A. *Heather@gmail.com* 617-555-1212	Ana E. *Ana@aol.com* ??
	Jose B. *Jose@gmail.com* 718-555-1212	Mark F. *Mark@aol.com* 908-555-1212
Swing	Rose C. *rose@gmail.com* 206-555-1212	Charlie G. *Charlie@gmail.com* 434-555-1212
	Brad D. *brad@aol.com* 808-555-1212	Laura H. ?? ??

Download this at
*labornotes.org/
secrets*

Whew! You've found yourself some allies. You've got a good handle on who's who in the workplace, how the groups function, and who their leaders are. Now it's time to figure out what makes a good issue to organize around.

That might sound strange. You were probably drawn to organizing in the first place because you were fired up about a burning issue at work. But burning as it may be, it might not be the best place to start. Organizers learn how to pick their battles. That's what we'll discuss in **Lesson 4: Choosing an Issue.**

LESSON 4:
CHOOSING AN ISSUE

In many workplace situations, the issue chooses you. Management is doing something awful and you feel the need to stop it: too much overtime, an unfair rule, discrimination.

But maybe there are so many problems where you work, you hardly know where to begin. You're angry about a lot of things. You sense that others are angry too—but maybe about different issues than you are.

If you're thinking long-term, you want to get beyond solving just one problem. You want to create an atmosphere where people feel and exercise their power, so anyone can nip problems in the bud. You want to make the union a living presence in the workplace.

Your first fight should reinforce the organizing impulse and give people confidence to go further.

THE RIGHT TO PRAY

Teamsters Local 117

When organizers from the Service Employees and the Teamsters started reaching out to airport workers in SeaTac, Washington, "we faced a big challenge," Jonathan Rosenblum recalled.

"The single largest group of low-wage airport workers hailed from Somalia. While their conditions were lousy, they weren't quite ready to trust us."

Workers in a few areas of the airport were union already. But the unions weren't seen as particularly responsive to African workers, especially Muslims. Years earlier, when Hertz Rent-a-Car suspended a group of Somali shuttle drivers for going to pray, it was an immigrant rights group—not their union— that filed a discrimination complaint to win back their jobs.

Praying five times a day is mandatory for observant Muslims. Finally Hertz management agreed to treat prayer breaks (which last only a few minutes) like a smoke break or a bathroom break: just take it and come back to work, no clock-out necessary. The company even provided a spare room for prayer.

When management decided to push back on the prayer breaks, the union got another chance to do the right thing.

One day when workers went to pray as usual, the manager told them to clock out. Shuttle driver Zainab Aweis recalled her manager standing with his arms extended, blocking the prayer room. "If you guys pray, you go home," he declared.

The workers appealed to their union, Teamsters Local 117. This time the union organized a multi-faith pray-in at the Hertz counter and invited the media.

It was a great organizing issue, as well as a righteous fight.

"Muslims, Christians, and Jews joined union and community activists, praying while holding signs that read, 'Respect me, respect my religion,'" Rosenblum wrote. "Union officers and the Hertz shop steward went on national news shows. They brought in lawyers.

"You can imagine the negative blowback the Teamsters got—locally, from some of their members, and also in the national blogosphere. But their willingness to take on this fight proved to be a turning point in the relationship between the unions at the airport and the East African community.

"After the pray-in, community doors began to open. We were invited to conduct union meetings in the mosques. Imams delivered Friday sermons exhorting people to get civically involved. Workers warmed up to organizers at the airport, saying, 'I heard you were at the mosque,' or 'The imam told us about the union.' The airport campaign gained momentum."

Two years later, when the unions worked to pass a ballot initiative for a $15 minimum wage in SeaTac, these relationships were crucial. The campaign registered 900 new voters in the small city—almost all of them new immigrants or children of immigrants.

"Probably more than 200 were registered outside Friday prayers," Rosenblum says. "We won the ballot initiative by 77 votes."

Working Washington

STRIKING A CHORD

The Teamster local leaders who organized the pray-in at Hertz didn't set out to pick a good issue and organize around it. They just reacted on principle when they saw that members' rights were being violated.

But as it turned out, this problem struck a deep chord with a group of members who hadn't felt much positive connection with the union before. The people who got involved discovered values in common. They formed new relationships of mutual respect and trust.

It *was* a great organizing issue, as well as a righteous fight.

The same principles hold true when you're looking to get things going in any workplace. The next four secrets are your criteria for picking a good organizing issue.

Download this at
*labornotes.org/
secrets*

A GOOD ORGANIZING ISSUE...

- is widely felt

- is deeply felt

- is winnable

- builds the union and builds leaders

#22
CHOOSE AN ISSUE THAT'S WIDELY FELT

TWU Local 100

How common is the problem? How many workers face this situation?

Many people must feel that this is a real problem and agree with the solution you're pursuing. If it affects only a handful of workers on the third shift who nobody else ever sees, it's probably not the best place to start.

When managers in New York City's bikeshare system announced new schedules for mechanics, it didn't take long to spot a widely felt issue. "Everyone went ballistic," said organizer Nick Bedell.

No matter which schedule you picked, you would be forced to work a weekend day. No one wanted to work weekends—and they didn't see why they should. Their job was to repair a fleet of bicycles that generally broke at a predictable rate. Fixing them Monday through Friday was working fine.

The mechanics, who had recently formed a union with Transport Workers Local 100, wrote up a protest petition, boycotted the picking procedure, and pushed for alternative schedules. They won.

Beware of an issue that pits one group of union members against another. If such a conflict has everyone fired up, but on different sides, look for the underlying problem that management is causing, and a solution both groups can get behind.

SHOW THAT MANY PEOPLE CARE

When petitioning, have signers write down their department, so everyone can see the breadth of support.

At a hospital, nurses got two blank books and wrote in them about a certain issue, signing their quotes. They took the books around the hospital to demonstrate that support was growing and to get more nurses to write their quotes in the books.

Next, the nurses made huge posters proclaiming their support, with their pictures and signatures. They left blank spaces for new supporters and took the posters to meetings where people could add their pictures.

#23

CHOOSE AN ISSUE THAT'S DEEPLY FELT

Is this an issue that people feel strongly enough about to actually do something?

Is this an issue that people feel strongly enough about to actually do something? It's not enough that many people agree, if none are really hot under the collar.

Chele Fulmore, a Teamster steward at UPS, tells of the time management changed the rules for taking lunch—and fired a worker for not fully understanding the new procedure.

His fellow workers were infuriated. No one else understood the procedure, either, and now the stakes were high. Everyone feared messing up and losing their jobs.

So most of the drivers signed a petition saying that the manager had never explained the new rule, which made him look incompetent to his superiors. The fired worker got his job back.

The Hertz pray-in is another great example. The issue mattered profoundly to the workers affected, and to their whole community. It wasn't just about breaks. It was about their religious faith.

Organizer Ahmed Ali reflected afterwards that it's these kinds of underlying values—faith, justice, human dignity, freedom of speech—that can "hold us together in the long run."

COULD THIS GRIEVANCE BE AN ORGANIZING ISSUE?

If you're a union steward, people bring you their workplace problems all the time.

After listening to a concern, you probably ask them to take a series of steps: write up the facts, identify which contract provisions are being violated, go with you to talk with the supervisor, and if the problem isn't resolved, work with you to file a grievance. All good steps.

But there's one more question you should always ask: "Anyone else in the same situation?"

"That question could change everything," says organizer Ellen David Friedman. You could be on your way to finding an issue that's *widely and deeply felt.*

Not every grievance will turn out to be a good organizing issue, of course. But if the worker thinks others may be affected, ask her to talk with co-workers and keep track of what she finds out.

If others are concerned too, she should get them together to talk about how to solve the problem. Maybe this should be a group grievance, presented to the supervisor by a whole delegation. It could be the seed of an action campaign.

Read more in *The Steward's Toolbox.*

#24

CHOOSE AN ISSUE THAT'S WINNABLE

It's hard to know for sure whether you *will* win, but it's possible to have a good idea whether you *can*.

"If you are a new group, you want to err on the side of choosing an easy issue," says organizer Marsha Niemeijer. "You want to bring more people in, so you need to have a win, to inspire those who will be skeptical. You want people to learn that they can make a difference."

> You need to have a win, to inspire those who will be skeptical.

So your group should match your demand to the power you've already got. Ask these questions:

- **What do we want?** You need to agree on a definition of what a "win" is, so your group should talk early on about what you consider an acceptable solution, including compromises.

- **Who can say yes?** Assess exactly who can fix the problem. Is it a lower-level manager, or that manager's boss, or is it the CEO? "If it's the CEO," Niemeijer says, "you've got a long way to go." Managers' personalities, past history, prejudices, and stubbornness will come into this assessment, too.

Stand Up to Verizon

- **For the decision-maker, what's the price of saying yes?** Consider the dollars and cents, but also how much the manager has riding on the issue politically or personally. Is this an issue that she feels strongly about and wouldn't want to lose face over? If she gave in, would it cause her other problems?

Could you imagine her giving in simply so that workers would stop bugging her? You might be surprised how often managers have some wiggle room. They just haven't been pressed on the issue.

Assess exactly who can fix the problem.

Have workers in other departments ever won on this issue? If so, you have a precedent.

Management gave in and the sky didn't fall. How did those workers win?

- **How high can you push the price of saying no?** How many people will be willing to do something, and how far will those people go? Take into account who's affected by the problem, how strongly they feel about it, what actions they've taken in the past, and whether the relevant leaders are on board with your plan.

To win, you'll need to make it harder for the decision-maker to keep saying no than to say yes. Would that take five people marching into the office together, 25 signing a petition, or a majority threatening to strike? The more pressure you can bring to bear, the more issues will become winnable.

To win, you'll need to make it harder for the decision-maker to keep saying no than to say yes.

THE MONEY WAS THERE

A public employee union in New Jersey was negotiating a first contract for group-home workers who made $9 an hour. They found out that the state government, which funded the group homes, had budgeted $1 an hour to raise workers' pay.

The money was there—but management hadn't passed it along. That gave the workers confidence that they could win. They made up a chant about the director of the program, a Mr. Diminot, and protested outside management's offices:

"Hi ho, Dimonot, we've been looking high and low. Our dollar, where is our dollar?"

During a softball game that managers participated in, workers organized a scavenger hunt for the dollar. They pinned a dollar to their shirts and wore them to work on Solidarity Fridays. Together, they filled out charts of things they would have done if they had gotten the dollar, and faxed them to management.

When the contract was signed, workers did not get a dollar—they got $1.60.

SHORT-TERM AND LONG-TERM GOALS

Fight for 15

You should usually pick the low-hanging fruit for your first target. But a small, winnable fight could work in tandem with a big, not-yet-winnable one.

Read more like this in *Labor Notes* magazine.

Niemeijer gives the example of hospital nurses who are simultaneously fighting for a tougher goal, more staffing, and an easier one, keeping more supplies on hand. Management "won't fix staffing yet," she says, "but they will fix supplies—and it's partly because they know we will continue to pressure them about staffing. They think they can distract us from our bigger goal by giving in on our small one."

Fast-food workers across the country have staged walkouts and rallies for very high goals: a $15 minimum wage and a union. But in the middle of that long-term campaign, at a McDonald's in Manhattan, workers took action on a more easily winnable issue.

One scorching July day, a worker fainted from the heat. The crew walked out, quickly drawing press attention because fast-food workers were already in the news. Workers told reporters the air conditioning had been broken for at least nine years. The franchise owner showed up with a fix the same afternoon.

A small, winnable fight could work in tandem with a big, not-yet-winnable one.

CHOOSE AN ISSUE THAT BUILDS THE UNION

Consider how this fight will build your capacity for future fights:

- Will the issue attract leaders or groups who haven't been very involved?
- Will it build solidarity between groups?
- Will it give you the chance to try an action that's one step beyond what you've done before?
- Will the solution lay the groundwork for future improvements?

At a Los Angeles hospital, stewards were demoralized—and few and far between. They got together to make a plan to find more leaders and rebuild their union.

They wanted their first organizing issue to be a good one. After meeting for weeks, they boiled down their criteria. They would pick a small work area of 10 to 30 workers where there was a problem that people felt strongly about, and where at least one leader was already a union activist or had the potential to become one.

It was getting close to December, and management announced that workers who were sick for even one

California Nurses Association

day that month would have to bring a doctor's note. Longstanding policy had been to require a note only for a three-day absence.

Bingo! People were furious. In one ward with 27 workers, people wrote up a petition asking for a meeting with management; everyone signed it. The group asked management to meet with 12 to 15 people.

"Management said, 'You've got to be kidding, we're short-staffed,'" organizer Paul Krehbiel remembers. Managers agreed to meet with four.

But soon after the meeting started, two more people came down from the ward to join in. "We're on our break," they said. The six workers took turns explaining how the new policy would cause them problems.

Consider how this fight will build your capacity for future fights.

"Managers kept looking nervously at their watches, and after 15 minutes they said that the workers on break had to return to the ward," says Krehbiel. "I told management they were going to return, but first they needed to tell their story.

"As they were telling their stories, two more workers began their breaks and came into the meeting… Management was clearly upset. 'Those first two workers have to go back now,' they said emphatically. 'Their break is over. We can't have so many people off the ward at once.'

"'We know,' we responded, 'he's just finishing up now.' Then the worker talked another two or three minutes."

The meeting lasted two hours, with most of the department rotating through. "We pushed the envelope as much as possible," Krehbiel says, "to have people stay in the meeting as long as they could."

Los Angeles Raise the Wage

The action was a success—management lightened up on the doctor's note policy. And because so many people had participated, it was a success at building the union, too. One new steward was recruited, and three new people volunteered to work with her.

DEFENDING BREAKS

If management is infringing on your breaks, you could print up small cards with the contract clause that guarantees break time, and hand the card to any supervisor who tries to guilt-trip someone into skipping her break.

Or a big group could all go on break at exactly the same time one day. Or they could walk through the worksite ringing a bell or blowing whistles to announce break time.

#26 EVEN WHEN YOU LOSE, YOU GAIN SOMETHING

Jim Levitt

At the end of the day, from each battle we want three things:

- **Victory.** Did we get a solid improvement in our working conditions?

- **Lessons learned.** Did we get smarter about the forces we're facing and what it will take to win? Did we hone our tactical skills or our understanding of strategy?

- **A stronger organization.** Did we build personal connections of trust, or alliances that can be used again? Have more leaders stepped forward?

Each fight should build off the last. It often happens that we don't win the concrete gain we wanted, but we do come out smarter and better organized—which makes it more likely we can win next time.

It's an organizer's job to point out to co-workers what was won: "We didn't get our breaks back this time, but now that we have all those connections on night shift that we didn't have before, let's start thinking about how we can try again."

Most people are only looking for the first kind of win—the immediate change they can see. Pay attention to consolidating the lessons and the organization, too.

Each fight should build off the last.

WHY GRIEVANCES ARE NOT ENOUGH

Hawaii Teachers Work to the Rules

If only we could count on contract enforcement to keep our workplaces trouble-free.

But every time management gets a chance, it will encroach into territory the union has won, taking away things we thought the contract protected. The contract reflects the balance of power between management and workers at the moment it was signed—but not necessarily the balance today.

Simply filing a grievance doesn't build power. It's not usually a collective activity. While the grievance moves from step to step, the members have nothing to do but wait.

Besides, grievances can fix only a tiny fraction of the injustices that go on in any workplace. Think about the individual workers whose rights are violated. Most won't file a grievance. Some are still on probation, or already facing discrimination, or simply afraid they'll be marked as troublemakers. Some don't realize they have the right to grieve.

Simply filing a grievance doesn't build power.

Even a good steward can't comb the shop getting all the shy or fearful workers to submit their grievances. In any case, the steward wouldn't have time to file them all; she has to pick her battles.

So of the many grievances that might have been filed, only a handful actually are. Months later, a few are finally won, but only the workers involved ever know about them. Even those with similar problems may not realize that a grievance happened. Most are left stewing over wrongs that go unaddressed.

That's why this book teaches you how to back up grievances with shop floor action or bypass the grievance system altogether. There still won't be time to address every issue—but the more people participate in solving a problem, the more they will develop the skills and confidence to take on other problems, and the union's power will grow.

You're developing a union culture in the workplace—not just at the union hall—where people expect to participate in defending the contract and defending each other.

Download this at
*labornotes.org/
secrets*

EXERCISE:
EVALUATE AN ORGANIZING ISSUE

Have you started mulling over some possible organizing issues at your workplace? Pick one, and answer these questions to help you think through its organizing potential.

1. **What's the problem?**

2. **What's our proposed solution?**

3. **Is this issue widely felt?**
   - How many people are technically affected by the problem?
   - How many people *feel* like it affects them?

4. **Is it deeply felt?**
   - How much do people care about this issue?
   - What are they willing to do about it?

5. **Is it winnable?**
   - Who's the decision-maker who could say yes to our solution?
   - What would it cost this person to say yes? Consider not just the budget but also the decision-maker's personal or political investment in the issue.
   - How much pressure will we have to bring to overcome this person's resistance?

- Who's already involved in organizing on this issue? Who would need to get involved?

- How far are members willing to go on this issue—far enough to win?

6. How will this fight build the union?

- Will it teach members a new lesson or skill, or give us a chance to go one step farther than we've gone before?

- Will it involve groups or leaders who are underrepresented in our organizing so far?

- Will it build solidarity between groups?

- Will the solution set a good precedent for future fights?

Download this at
labornotes.org/secrets

Now you know how to pick the right issue. In **Lesson 5: An Escalating Campaign,** you'll learn how to make an action plan to push management to address your goal.

LESSON 5: AN ESCALATING CAMPAIGN

Once you've identified the issue, potential leaders, and your target, you can think about tactics that will get you what you want. This lesson tells how to choose your tactics and deploy them in the right order as part of an escalating campaign.

We'll begin with a story that shows how to start with low-intensity tactics and turn up the heat. It happened in a local that had not been in good shape. Grievances were rare, and union meetings were nonexistent. But a handful of teachers at one school got together and figured out how to get results.

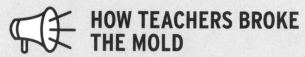

HOW TEACHERS BROKE THE MOLD

"Our school was old and had not been well maintained," writes Steve Hinds, who was a teacher in New Haven, Connecticut. "We noticed that many teachers were suffering from sinus problems, headaches, and other respiratory illnesses. A group of teachers met to decide what to do.

"We decided to file a grievance, and got over 90 percent of the teachers to sign it in a single day. While gathering the signatures, we also conducted a health survey, and found that more than 70 percent suffered from symptoms related to air quality.

"There had been little grievance activity for years, so we could start fresh." The teachers formed a Grievance Committee, welcoming anyone. It held weekly meetings, produced a newsletter, and kept in daily contact with the parents' organization.

Using an information request, the committee forced the city to hand over a study of the school's air quality. "The report showed that the city knew there was a mold infestation in our building," Hinds writes.

"Our demands were simple. We wanted the city to do what its own report concluded it should have done six months earlier—fix the roof leaks that let moisture in, remove moldy ceiling tiles, and clean the walls and floors with bleach solution.

"We gave the city a deadline to agree to a reasonable completion date, followed by a walk-through by teachers and parents to inspect the completed work.

"The city indicated it was working on the problems, but wasn't formally agreeing to anything."

So the teachers decided to organize a meeting with parents. To publicize it, the next day teachers wore surgical masks to school.

"What a day it was," Hinds remembers. "We didn't even need to call the newspapers and TV stations to attract attention. Word got out through student cell phones, and the cameras and reporters were at the school doors by 9 a.m.

"Parents who heard about the masks were calling downtown with their concerns. City officials were furious, and the superintendent showed up to bully us. Most of the teachers simply walked out of this meeting.

"The city agreed to our timetable by the end of the day. The following day, a crew went through the building room by room to create a master list of work to be done. This list led to some 1,000 work orders. More work was done to improve our school building in those few months than had been done in the previous two decades, and health complaints by teachers and students gradually eased."

Through this campaign, Hinds wrote, "we developed leadership and negotiating skills in 15 members who previously had had no experience. And we built credibility with parents, who saw that the union was not interested only in salaries. We went on to form a Contract Organizing Group to pressure the local to fight for smaller classes."

#27 ACTIONS SPEAK LOUDER THAN WORDS

Dennis Williams, United Steelworkers

How do we address a problem in the workplace? The usual answer, if we have a union, is to file a grievance, setting paperwork in motion.

But the grievance procedure can be invisible, slow, and fruitless. And many problems aren't technically grievances. They're simply the result of someone else having power over you.

To solve the school mold problem, Steve Hinds and the other teachers started with a grievance—but they didn't end there. They turned up the heat with a series of actions that built their group's unity and confidence, culminating in the day everyone wore surgical masks to school and walked out of a meeting with the superintendent.

Whether or not a grievance is part of our plan, we're more likely to win if we take action on the job. Our actions should be:

- **Visible and public**, so that members are aware of what is taking place and the result.

- **Collective**, involving as many members as possible.

- **Confrontational**, mobilizing members to face the decision-makers who have the power to resolve the problem.

"Not only does worksite mobilization work, it shifts the power for the next fight," says Hetty Rosenstein, longtime president of a public employees union in New Jersey.

"When workers confront management at the worksite, and as a result they correct something that is wrong, or they improve their conditions, or they get a fired worker reinstated, a power shift occurs right before their eyes.

"It happens in real time and workers witness it. Management holds the power over the situation— and workers take it away."

> Mobilizing not only gets results, but also shifts power for the next fight.

#28

MAKE A GAME PLAN

Once you've identified a good organizing issue (see Lesson 4), you need a plan of action.

THE THREE BASICS OF A PLAN

1. **What exactly do you want?** It's amazing how far along folks can be in a campaign without having identified what solution they're after, and whether or not it's winnable. The teachers had clear demands for how the city could fix the mold problem.

2. **Who has the power to fix the problem?** It's not enough to say "management." Figure out which person in management could say yes to your solution. The teachers zeroed in on decision-makers at the city level.

3. **Which tactics can work?** Aim your actions to build the pressure on the decision-maker you've identified. Consider how much pressure it will take to win, and where your leverage is.

GETTING BUY-IN

To get people on board, your strategy must be clear and credible—people have to understand it and believe it can work. Practice explaining the plan simply and quickly.

#29

HOLD SMALL MEETINGS

New people are more likely to come to a small meeting.

You might have the impulse to start by inviting everyone in the workplace to a meeting. It's natural to think "strength in numbers" and assume people will feel more confident if they can see lots of people in the same room. But that's not likely to happen at the beginning of your campaign, and it doesn't have to be a goal.

Instead, said Andrew Tripp, who helped organize a union in a big Vermont hospital, "new people are more likely to come to a small meeting that includes a friend or co-worker they know. And at that meeting, they are more likely to participate than at a large meeting where their presence has little impact.

"You cannot have a conversation at a large meeting. But you can in a small meeting, and you can build a relationship." (Remember Lesson 2: relationships are key.)

Read more in *A Troublemaker's Handbook 2.*

When you're starting out, a "small meeting" may be as small as two people. According to Tripp, that's how workers won their organizing drive: "We had small meetings with 670 nurses who gave us a verbal commitment to the union, and we got 672 yes votes out of about 1,000 cast."

FIVE PEOPLE CAN DO A LOT

Members of Rising Stars, the young worker committee of Office and Professional Employees Local 2 in Washington, D.C., learned a similar lesson when they were first getting started.

Their first meeting drew 10 excited people. But the group "got bogged down in the ins and outs of trying to get started," said organizer Caniesha Seldon. So people "trickled off."

"We kept waiting for more people [to join]," Seldon said. "Then you lost the ones you had because you're waiting and not giving them anything to do."

She learned from the experience, though. The group was revived the next year and is now going strong.

"A lot of people start with really big expectations when they send out a meeting notice, and get really disappointed when only five people show up," said Seldon. "But a dedicated group of five people can do a lot of things. People will see what you're doing if you keep doing it."

People will see what you're doing, if you keep doing it.

GETTING THE BALL ROLLING

Say there's a problem where you work. Maybe you have a supervisor who humiliates someone in front of co-workers. You've tried reasoning with him, but nothing changes. You want to do something.

- **Think clearly about the problem** you're facing. Try to get past the emotion—the anger, resentment, shame, or whatever you're feeling about it. Write down the simple facts.

- **Resist the urge** to act only on emotion, or to do something all by yourself. That's often when you're most vulnerable, and you might make more trouble for yourself than for the boss. Instead, take a deep breath and reach out to co-workers.

- **Find someone at work you trust**, and share the facts you've written down. Ask for an honest opinion. If you both agree that this is a serious problem, see if you can come up with the names of other co-workers who are affected, too.

- **Talk one on one** with these other people. So far, you're just checking to see if others agree with you, not deciding what you're going to do about it.

- **Some people will be more concerned than others.** Don't be discouraged. Keep talking—without pestering people—until you find even one person who shares your desire to do something.

- **If you find a small handful of co-workers** who share this problem, get them together, perhaps over a cup of coffee during your break. First share your fears about what could happen if your group did something. Then, talk about what will happen if you do nothing. This will usually help make up your mind to do something! Then start talking about steps you could take.

- **Figure out together** who in management is the decision-maker on the issue. Does this boss know about the problem? How could you approach the boss, collectively? What are the risks and advantages of different approaches?

- **Check your workplace map** from Lesson 3. Think about who's involved so far, and who else you'll need to involve in order to win. Are there key leaders you want to involve early on? Who in your group should approach them, and what approach might work best?

- **Use the information** in Lessons 4 and 5 to make a plan. Take small steps to build your trust as a group. This is the best way to overcome fear.

Download this at
*labornotes.org/
secrets*

#30 EVERY BOSS HAS A WEAK SPOT

Coalition of Immokalee Workers

Think about where your employer is vulnerable.

Steel production in the late 1800s used to require one crucial step: a 20-minute process called the "blow" that removed impurities, strengthening the metal. It was not unheard of for union members to go to the supervisor at the start of the blow and demand that some important grievance be resolved.

According to old-timers, it was amazing what the company could accomplish in those 20 minutes. These workers had found their employer's vulnerability—and they used it to make the workplace safer and more humane.

Think about where your employer is vulnerable. For some companies it might be their logo or their image, which they have spent millions of dollars cultivating. For others it might be a bottleneck in the production process, or a weakness in their just-in-time inventory system.

WHISTLE WHILE YOU WORK

At a Fortune 500 truck factory, supervisors were ruthless and degrading. Discipline was arbitrary and unjust. At the monthly union meeting one worker noted that they were all being "railroaded."

A few weeks later, 2,000 plastic whistles shaped like locomotives arrived at the local. The instructions were simple: whenever you can see a supervisor on the shop floor, blow your whistle.

At first, whistles were going off all over. But by the morning break the plant floor was quiet. Not a single supervisor dared to show his face.

The next day in contract bargaining, the employer refused to bargain until the whistles were removed. The bargaining team noted the company's statements on refusing to bargain, and asked for a break to go call the Labor Board.

Bargaining resumed immediately, with positive results.

 **LUNCH TO RULE**

On a military base, aircraft maintenance workers would happily interrupt their lunch in order to deal with urgent problems. But in return they had an understanding that, once the problem was solved, they would go back to their sandwiches even though the lunch period had ended.

The situation was mutually acceptable for several years—until a new supervisor came along. We all know how that is. Had to prove himself. Show who's boss. Etc.

'Okay, we'll play by your rules.'

Steve Eames, an international rep for the Boilermakers union, explained that the new supervisor insisted that workers take their lunch between 12:00 and 12:30, period.

"So the steward said, 'Okay, we'll play by the rules,'" Eames remembers. The maintenance workers had previously eaten at a lunch table in the work area. But now, when 12 o'clock came, they left and went to a fast-food restaurant on the base. For three or four days they all went as a group, leaving the shop unattended.

One day a plane came in during the half-hour lunch period. No one was there to help bring the plane in, or to check it out. The supervisor had to park the plane by himself.

"The boss went and talked to the steward, and the steward said, 'That's our time, we're at lunch,'" said Eames. "'You got what you wanted.'"

The workers went out for lunch for a couple more days, and then they ended what we might call "lunch to rule." "They didn't want to file a grievance," says Eames, "because the company would have won on the basis of contract language.

"Without anything in writing, it went back to the way it had been before. It empowered the guys. It told the supervisor, we'll be a little flexible if you'll be flexible."

Lunch to rule.

Read more like this in *Labor Notes* magazine.

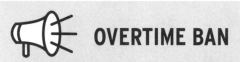

OVERTIME BAN

Jim West, *jimwestphoto.com*

At a machine tool shop in Vermont, the company put in a harsh new absentee policy. Workers responded with a nine-month refusal to work overtime.

For nine months, workers refused to work overtime.

Union officials and stewards did not organize the ban, which under many union contracts could be illegal. "There was always another level of union leadership that did not hold any official position," says David Cohen, who was a representative for the United Electrical Workers at the time.

"Mostly, the unofficial leaders were the older workers—the mentors, if you will—who had the respect of the others. They did not hold formal meetings. They just talked amongst themselves and to the elected leaders.

The unofficial leaders were the older workers who had respect of the others.

"They did the work the elected leaders could not do. In fact, the union officials sometimes worked overtime, to make it clear that the ban was not official policy. It really was a rank-and-file effort.

"During the overtime ban, the union committee spent months negotiating over the absentee program, making it as loose as possible. Then we got workers to file grievances over every point they received for being late or absent. The only rule was that workers had to go to the grievance meeting and argue their case at the first step. This made it clear to the company that the members were opposed to the program.

"At one point there were hundreds of grievances pending. The union committee was spending eight hours a day meeting with the company. This in itself represented a big loss in production.

"Eventually, without ever admitting that the absentee plan was a failure, the company stopped enforcing it and installed new time clocks that could give workers a reasonable grace period."

KEEP THE BOSS OFF BALANCE

Managers like routine. They like to know that what happened yesterday will happen today and that no one is thinking too hard about it. You can make them nervous simply by doing something different, even something normal that would be unthreatening to the non-managerial mind. When they have to keep guessing where the next shot is coming from, you have the upper hand.

POWERFUL WAYS TO ACT

- **Disrupt the flow of work**, the chain of command, or the employer's control over workers. Disruption gets attention, and often gets results.

- **Alter and improve.** Some things we can change simply by doing them differently: slow down production, take a longer break, or change the way work is organized. Once something is changed, it's harder for the employer to change it back.

- **Take control.** When the boss gives an order, he sets a chain of events in motion. When we act collectively, we start a chain of events in a different direction.

Jim West, *jimwestphoto.com*

"The corporate culture is not a creative culture," says Joe Fahey, a former Teamster leader, "and we need to look at that as an opportunity.

Management is more easily scared than we realize.

"I used to bargain with Smuckers," Fahey recalls. "We decided to do things that would freak them out. Factory life is very predictable. The workers decided to take their breaks at the railroad tracks, instead of at the same table and the same bench that they did every day. It was easy for the workers to do, but it was scary for management. They are more easily scared than we realize."

In another Teamsters plant, newly elected leaders of the local were bargaining with management for the first time. None had been to college or had union experience, and they were intimidated.

"We wanted to set it up to make the company feel at least as uncomfortable at the first meeting as the workers feel," Fahey said. "The first negotiations were in the local union hall, so we had an opportunity to set the stage. We arranged the chairs in a circle, with no table. We invited the management team in and pointed to the empty chairs and said, 'Have a seat.'

"It worked. They were polite but looked really uncomfortable. Their eyes were rolling. They had no place to open their briefcases or their laptops. They were not sure what to do with their legs.

"Now that we had made them uncomfortable, we tried to put them at ease. We said, 'We want you to get to know us a bit and we want to get to know you a bit. We all have different jobs. You probably know more about our jobs than we know about your jobs. So let's go around the circle and introduce ourselves.'

"When it got to the plant manager, we asked him what he did and who his boss was. This company makes frozen snacks. He answered, 'My job is to make sure the lines produce 132 snacks per minute.' We asked him more questions and he went on and on, like he was enjoying the fact that someone was asking him a question.

"He eventually revealed some things that the human relations manager didn't like, and the human relations manager rapped him on the head with his knuckles and said, 'You shared too much! You shared too much!'"

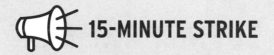 **15-MINUTE STRIKE**

Pennsylvania social workers figured out how to catch management off guard. During negotiations with the state, spokesman Ray Martinez said, "we wanted an activity that would irritate the boss, educate the public, and at the same time get the members psyched up. We decided that we would all take our 15-minute breaks at the same time."

The union used its phone trees to call members at home. "At the agreed date and time," Martinez says, "all of our members would get up and walk out of the office. This meant that clients in the office, phone calls, and so on would be placed on hold. In other words, all activity ceased.

"This served a couple of purposes. First, management and clients would get a feel for what it would be like without our services if we were to go on strike. Secondly, we, the members, would be outside of the worksite having outdoor shop meetings and updating the workers on the latest on the negotiations.

"While this was going on, we had picket signs asking drivers to honk their horns to show us their support. The beauty of it all was that this was perfectly legal, so there was nothing management could do."

At the end of the 15-minute break, everybody went back inside and went back to work.

#32

TURN UP THE HEAT

Don't bring out your big guns right away. Start with an easy-to-do activity that won't take a whole lot of commitment on the part of your co-workers. If enough people participate, you've built communication and solidarity. Maybe you've had some fun.

As your actions grow more intense, managers begin to understand you mean business.

Take the New Haven teachers' fight against mold, for example. They began by gathering signatures on a grievance and doing a health survey. This helped them verify how widely and deeply felt their issue was, and form a network of activists who would lead their co-workers through the campaign.

If you don't achieve your goal through your first step, you then try something that's a bit harder, that pushes the boss a bit more. If necessary, another step could be to threaten to bring in outside pressure or publicity. And so on.

Why escalate gradually?

- **Take the high road.** By starting small, you show you are reasonable and credible. You *did* try asking politely.

- **It builds your group.** If you start off with low-intensity actions, members who have never said boo to the boss before will be more likely to participate. As your actions get more intense, make sure not to leave people behind.

- **Strength in numbers.** If you leap straight into high-intensity actions and only a few people participate, it's easy for your employer to single them out. With a few illegal disciplines, management can teach everyone the lesson that sticking your neck out means getting your head chopped off. If you start smaller and build, you can achieve greater participation.

- **Each action has a greater impact than the action before.** As your actions get more and more intense, managers begin to understand that you mean business. You also keep them guessing. When supervisors don't know what's going to happen next—that's when they make mistakes. And every time they make a mistake, the balance of power shifts in your direction.

- **Don't play your aces too soon.** If you do your worst first, there's nowhere for your campaign to go but down. It's more effective when managers can see there's a lot more to come—and there's still time to save themselves a headache by giving in.

ACTION THERMOMETER

One way to visualize escalating tactics is to arrange them on a thermometer, with each action "hotter" than the last. Here are the steps the New Haven teachers took to solve the mold problem at their school, beginning from the bottom of the thermometer:

- Enjoyed their victory

- Walked out of a meeting en masse

- Spoke to the media

- Pulled a publicity stunt

- Called a meeting of supporters

- Used the result to formulate specific demands, with deadlines

- Filed an information request

- Reached out to parents

- Published a newsletter

- Formed a grievance committee

- Developed a communication network

- Conducted a health survey

- Gathered signatures on a grievance

- Defined their issue: air quality

- Met as a small group

In many cases a survey would be the lowest-intensity task, the one to start with. But in this case teachers were already fired up about the mold issue, and the initial group had no trouble getting them to sign a group grievance.

When the teachers walked out on the superintendent, it showed how far they had come. Their escalating campaign had built up their sense of the justice of their cause, and they were not afraid.

Download this at
*labornotes.org/
secrets*

CHECKLIST: CHOOSE TACTICS THAT FIT

- Does the action relate to your issue?

- Will it increase the pressure on the decision-maker?

- Is it simple?

- Is it visible?

- Is it timed for effect?

- Is it new and different—or tried and true?

- Are enough people ready to do it?

- How will others react? Will it unify people?

- How will management react? Could it backfire?

- Does it violate the law or the contract? If so, are you prepared for the consequences?

- Will it be fun?

EXERCISE:
ARRANGE THESE TACTICS ON A THERMOMETER

Here's an assortment of tactics that workers have used and loved. Pick an issue in your workplace and imagine you're planning an escalating campaign. Draw a thermometer, and write in the tactics you might use, beginning at the bottom with the mildest ones.

Which tactics are "hotter" might vary from one workplace to another, and some tactics will be unique to a particular workplace. Can you think of actions you might try that aren't on this list? Place these on your thermometer, too.

Bombard the boss with phone calls and emails

Wear T-shirts or hats with a slogan or cartoon on a particular day

Strike

Put up posters

Visit the boss in a small group

Wear buttons or stickers

File a group grievance with signatures

Distribute leaflets

Hold an informational picket line

Set up a Facebook page for your campaign

Work to rule

Write and sing a song about the boss

Rally in the parking lot and enter the building at the same time

Circulate a petition

Barrage management with tweets and Facebook comments

Do a survey

Do a skit or other creative action at a picket line, shareholders' meeting, or public place

Invite a giant inflatable rat to sit outside the workplace

Stop working overtime, all together

Call the boss out in front of other workers

Meet with outside supporters; get them to take action, too

Make up wallet cards that define workers' rights

Everyone gets "sick" on the same day

Visit the boss in a large group

All take breaks at the same time

Rally at company headquarters or another target

Spill the beans to the media

#33

MAKE SURE EVERY JOB GETS DONE

Chicago Teachers Union

Even a tactic that sounds simple, like getting everyone to wear stickers on the same day, takes planning and follow-through.

Your group will need to identify all the tasks required, assign them to specific people, with deadlines, and follow up to make sure people do them. An easy way to think about it is, "*Who* will do *what* by *when*?"

To keep anything from falling through the cracks, make a chart like this one for every tactic that's part of your campaign. Write down *all* the steps needed for this tactic, and assign one or more people to each task.

TACTIC: STICKER DAY

Task	Who?	By When?
Talk with co-workers about having a sticker day. Decide if we have enough buy-in to proceed.	All committee members	October 16
Come up with a catchy slogan.	Britney and Ben	October 20
Design the sticker.	Ben	October 22
Raise the money to buy the stickers.	Al, Calvin, Maria, Tonya	October 22
Print up the stickers at a union copy shop.	Freddie	October 23
Make a plan for handing out the stickers. Who will cover which areas?	Britney, Tonya, Maria, Millie	October 23
Inform people of their right to wear stickers, and prep them on how management might react.	All committee members	October 24
Hand out the stickers.	All committee members	October 25
Wear the stickers.	Everyone	October 25
Meet afterwards to debrief how it went.	All committee members	October 25

Adapted from United Steelworkers

You're on your way now, with a plan to build pressure till you win your issue. But what kind of backlash can you expect from managers, once they catch on? As your campaign ramps up, how will you cope with roadblocks? That's what we'll tackle in **Lesson 6: Expect the Unexpected.**

LESSON 6: EXPECT THE UNEXPECTED

You've planned a great campaign with an escalating series of tactics. But your bosses aren't going to take it lying down. As soon as they realize you're up to something, they'll be taking countermeasures.

And besides management's roadblocks, you'll run into some hurdles with your co-workers, your fellow committee members—and even yourself.

Every organizing campaign has its rocky spots. In this lesson we offer some principles and practices for keeping everything on track.

⫷ THE POWER OF SONG

David McDonald, ATU 587

Organizer Joe Uehlein tells this story from a union drive at a Georgia meatpacking plant.

Organizers were encountering a great deal of fear. One of management's most effective scare tactics was sending in a slick-looking Atlanta-based union buster, who walked up and down the killing floor without saying a word. "This guy would show up in his three-piece suit and just exude power," said Uehlein.

"So I began thinking about how to fight this, and I remembered a song I had heard called 'The Union Buster.' It's a parody written by Paul McKenna to the tune of 'Oh Susannah,' and the chorus goes:

"He's a union-buster, the boss's trusty aide. He helps keep our employees overworked and underpaid."

"I always carry my guitar in my car, so I brought it in, taught the song to the organizing committee, and we recorded it."

At that time the company allowed workers to select the music that was played over the loudspeaker while they were working. The next time the union buster

Properly provoked, the adversary will make mistakes.

appeared on the shop floor, "The Union Buster" suddenly began playing throughout the plant.

"The guy just went nuts," recalls Uehlein. "The committee saw immediately how a single song could bust through that veneer of invincibility."

Predictably, by the following day, the company was no longer letting employees select the music. So the next time the consultant appeared, the workers began singing "The Union Buster."

That resulted in a rule against singing. On the union buster's next visit, the workforce was whistling the now-familiar tune. When whistling was banned, workers hummed.

Uehlein says: "In the course of one week we built strength and solidarity among that workforce. Workers learned that they could become a force by taking action on just that one small thing.

"Not only were we able to poke through management's shield of power, we were able to anticipate their response and plan our next moves. We illustrated the organizing principle that 'Properly goaded, the adversary will trip and make mistakes.'"

And workers at the plant won their union.

#34 DON'T LET THE BOSS TRIP YOU UP

Jon Flanders

Managers always use the same playbook. They'll try to undermine your organizing with the same basic obstacles we talked about in Lesson 1:

FEAR

Management may create an atmosphere of tension. For instance, surveillance may increase.

Help co-workers find the courage to overcome their fear.

Outside consultants or high-level executives not usually spotted on the shop floor may suddenly appear. Managers may make threats, or even make an example of someone—though if they're smart, they recognize the risk of going too far and sparking a wave of anger.

Help co-workers find the courage to overcome their fear by tapping into their righteous anger over workplace injustices. Humor can be a big help, too (as with the "Union Buster" song).

HOPELESSNESS

Management will spread the message that your organizing is a waste of time, the decision is made, and you don't have any power anyway. But the harder supervisors are working to counter your campaign, the greater the evidence that you do have power. Point this out to co-workers every chance you get.

You'll be amazed at the myths management will circulate.

Inspire hope by formulating a credible plan to win. Start with small, winnable fights to help build your co-workers' confidence in the power of collective action.

CONFUSION

You'll be amazed at the creative rumors and myths management will start circulating to get people talking about anything but your issue. In a unionization drive, the standbys are "the union just wants your money," "the union can force you to go on strike," "the union will use your dues to support Democrats," and "the union will come between you and your supervisor." But who knows what else they'll dream up.

Centro de Trabajadores Unidos en Lucha

You can inoculate against the likeliest talking points, but you can't anticipate every lie. Instead, your job as an organizer is to share information and help interpret the boss's actions. Help your co-workers find clarity, not just about the facts, but also about why management is behaving this way.

DIVISION

Management may try to weaken your support by buying off particular leaders, offering a measly half-solution that only helps certain people, or pitting one group against another.

Promote unity by finding and emphasizing your common ground, usually the issue you're organizing

Help your co-workers interpret management's actions.

around. Look for opportunities to build relationships between groups, perhaps in a social setting. Agree ahead of time that all groups will discuss whatever offer management comes up with—no one will make any side deals.

WHOSE MEETING? OUR MEETING!

If management calls a mandatory meeting, how can rank and filers take the floor and take it over? You could do it with humor.

In one campaign, worker activists stood at the door handing out their own version of a meeting agenda, including suggested questions to ask.

In another, everyone in the meeting held a lollipop with the message, "We're not suckers."

TO REACT, OR NOT TO REACT?

ATU Local 836

Remember, your campaign won't be won with dueling flyers.

If management puts out a "fact sheet" filled with lies, how should you respond? It can be tempting to thoroughly refute every point, but you should stop and think before going down that rabbit hole.

Management is trying to distract and confuse. If derailing works, they'll keep it up, supplying more lies as quickly as you can debunk them. When you're on the defensive, you are—for the moment—losing.

Avoid dignifying an attack with a written response. Co-workers may be looking to you for cues on whether to take it seriously. You want to keep the focus on your issues, not their attacks.

So when should you react? Essentially, when you have to. If management is successfully changing the subject, then you may need to respond to what they're saying, in your flyers and conversations. The goal is to put out the fire and bring the focus back to your issues.

Remember, your campaign won't be won with dueling flyers, but with one-on-one conversations through the communication network you've been building. Management has enough money and personnel to out-flyer you, but you're the ones who are trusted shop floor leaders.

Do not respond to the boss's message just because:

- It's infuriating.
- It's a lie.

Do respond if:

- It's getting traction—people you care about are talking about it.
- It's closing people off to your message.

Download this at
*labornotes.org/
secrets*

 ANSWERING TOUGH QUESTIONS

On paper and in person, keep the focus on your message. When people come to you riled up over the spin from management, a good way to respond is "Affirm, Answer, Redirect."

Affirm: Let them know you're listening, you understand, and their feelings are valid. Your co-workers may be scared or upset by what they've heard. Don't get mad at them. It's management's fault, not theirs.

> *I hear you, I don't want to lose money either!*

Answer: Give a truthful, concise answer to the question. Don't be evasive. If there's a grain of truth to management's message, say that up front.

> *Yes, it's true we wouldn't be paid during a strike. Going on strike is a serious decision that requires a majority vote—so we only do it if most people decide it's worth it.*

If you don't know the answer, don't guess. Tell them you'll find out and get back to them. Make sure you follow through, to maintain trust.

Redirect: But once you've answered the question, don't get bogged down in too much back-and-forth about it. Instead, be ready with a question that brings the conversation back to your message and points out what management is trying to distract them from.

> *If they're so concerned about our pocketbooks all of a sudden, why haven't they given us a raise for two years?*

Remind your co-workers of the issues that inspired them to organize in the first place. Ask whether that's changed. Steer the conversation back to the plan to win, and the next steps.

 **EXERCISE:
PRACTICE ANSWERING TOUGH
QUESTIONS**

Pick a message management has used, or might use, to undermine your campaign. If there's a concern that's already been getting traction with your co-workers, use that one.

Write the concern the way a co-worker might phrase it. Now write what you would say to answer it, using the three steps:

- Affirm
- Answer
- Redirect

Practice out loud with a friend.

#35

PREPARE FOR THE WORST

Tim Dubnau

There's a reason why some people are afraid to stick their necks out. Management has been known to retaliate.

It's necessary to 'inoculate' folks about the retaliation that is sure to follow bold actions.

When Cablevision technicians in Brooklyn, New York, were fighting for their first contract, the company tried firing a key leader, Jerome Thompson. To defend him, 200 co-workers wore a sticker that simply said "Jerome." Forty stewards jammed into the vice president's office, demanding Thompson's job back. He was rehired with back pay the next day. The boss called it a misunderstanding.

Organizer Ellen David Friedman has seen a lot of this. It's necessary, she says, to "inoculate" folks about the retaliation that is sure to follow bold actions:

A fired union activist was rehired after 200 co-workers wore a sticker and 40 packed the supervisor's office.

Explain ahead of time that retaliation is expected. Do this at first in one-on-one conversations, and eventually in leaflets.

Spell out what it may look like. Some individuals may be singled out for "performance review" or written up for trumped-up infractions. Others could be penalized with new assignments, bad schedules, or malicious gossip. Someone could be suspended or fired.

Name it openly, to defuse the shame and fear that follows these sorts of attacks.

Describe the steps people should take if they become a target:

- The retaliation should be exposed by talking and writing about it.

- The facts should be mustered to build the case that this is retaliation for workplace activism.

- Supporters should be ready to protect the victimized co-worker with their own actions, such as petitions and buttons ("You can't scare us!"), a visit to the boss en masse, or filing grievances and unfair labor practice charges.

- If possible, identify and isolate any bosses who may be vulnerable. Analyze the power relations in the workplace. If a strong case can be made against a particular supervisor for bad behavior, upper-level executives may be willing to sacrifice that person to restore peace.

United Teachers Los Angeles

BEING AN ACTIVIST CAN PROTECT YOU

Kay Eisenhower, who was a clerk in an Oakland hospital, says, "Some workers might assume that being a steward or an activist tends to get one into trouble. But in general we had just the opposite experience.

"My co-workers believed that I was protected by my union role, that my aggressive, usually successful, representation of members ensured that I would not be personally targeted, and that if I were, the union would come in like a ton of bricks to defend me.

"I was able to point to myself as an example of how being outspoken didn't necessarily lead to trouble with management, as long as you did your job."

Being outspoken doesn't necessarily mean getting in trouble.

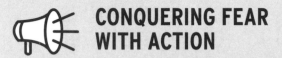

CONQUERING FEAR WITH ACTION

At a restaurant in Santa Fe, New Mexico, Carlos Campos and two co-workers formed a committee. The others in their workplace of 29 were too nervous to join.

In the past when they'd brought up working conditions, the boss would tell them, "the door's wide open and you can leave," said Campos.

The group's first public action was to hand their boss a letter, asking the restaurant to start paying for overtime, respect their lunch breaks, and stop requiring them to attend a monthly meeting without pay.

'Fear will always be there, but we have rights and we deserve respect.'

The restaurant fired all three. But with the help of a worker center, they filed a Labor Board complaint and organized a loud demonstration in front of the restaurant— a story that was picked up by local media.

In four months, Campos was back at work. The Labor Board had ordered the employer to reinstate him and his co-workers, and to reimburse all lost wages.

The restaurant also started providing lunch breaks, and ended the unpaid meetings and overtime.

"Fear will always be there, and employers take advantage of this," says Campos. "But we have rights and we deserve respect."

GO PUBLIC

The same worker center, Somos un Pueblo Unido, has supported the formation of 50 workplace committees at hotels, restaurants, car washes, landscapers, and cleaning companies.

Though Campos and his co-workers faced the worst retaliation a boss can dish out, Somos is finding that most employers, recognizing their legal position, don't retaliate at all.

The letter to the boss, signed by at least two workers, is crucial to bolster a legal defense. If workers are fired, they have clear documentation that they took part in collective action and the boss knew about it.

Equally important is staging a rally immediately after any retaliation. It draws publicity the boss doesn't want, and shows that the workers have community backing. Other employers, too, see what they'll face if they choose to retaliate.

All committee members must agree to speak to the media about their complaints. "If no one knows about this, we're not building power," says organizer Marcela Diaz.

WHEN YOU'RE CALLED INTO THE OFFICE

If managers start cornering individuals, how can you prepare people? Warn them what to expect. It's helpful to role-play how a one-on-one meeting might go.

Advise your co-workers that there's no need for heroics. Arguing with your supervisor about your campaign won't help. The supervisor's goal is either to intimidate you or to find out information, such as who the leaders are.

Here are some good practices to follow any time you are called into the office:

- **Assert your Weingarten rights.** If you have a legally recognized union in the private sector (even if you don't have a contract yet), you have the right to have a steward present in any meeting that could lead to discipline. (Many public sector unions have similar protections in state law or contracts.)

  So any time you start to feel intimidated, ask your supervisor directly: "Will this meeting lead to discipline?" If she says anything but "no"—including "yes," "maybe," "we'll see," or "I don't know yet"—tell her you want a steward present, as is your right.

- **Take notes on what the supervisor says**, especially if you think she might be violating your rights. (For instance, questions about your organizing could be illegal surveillance of union activity. Consult your union officers or a lawyer.)

Note-taking during the meeting could make the supervisor nervous enough to rein in her behavior—or it could make her mad enough to escalate. Gauge your particular supervisor. If not during the meeting, be sure to make a written record immediately afterward.

- **Answer questions** related to your work, but don't volunteer extra information you weren't asked.

- **Debrief soon afterwards** with a steward or core group member. This gives the steward a chance to make sure you're okay, find out if your rights were violated, answer any new fears or doubts management has planted, and gather intel on what management's up to.

Download this at
labornotes.org/
secrets

📢 WHEN RETALIATION FLOPS

At a Kroger supermarket in Virginia, management's attempt to retaliate backfired—and ended up encouraging co-workers to get involved with the union.

This supermarket had a glaring problem: a racist manager, who would discipline black workers for things white workers would not get in trouble for. When the weather was bad, black workers were sent outside to bring in carts. When there was a spill, black workers would be assigned to clean it up.

The pattern was clear. But at first just one person was ready to stand up against it—Laverne Wrenn, a shop steward.

Wrenn and her union representative started by taking the complaint to higher management, but the company refused to deal with it. So Wrenn started documenting the racist incidents herself—writing down each date and time, and identifying witnesses. She began calling out the manager every chance she got.

The manager tried retaliating against her, but Wrenn didn't back down. When she was passed over for a position she should have gotten by seniority, she filed a grievance and won. She got the position.

Something interesting began to happen. When other workers saw Wrenn standing up, many who'd never been interested in the union before came to her and signed up as members.

People were drawn in because they could see she was fighting on an issue they cared about. And the failed attempt to punish Wrenn had backfired. People saw that they weren't powerless. They started to think this fight was worth the risks— they might even win.

That's when one person's activism turned into a group organizing effort.

Soon many workers were helping to document everything the manager did. They put together a team from different departments and shifts to make sure they caught every incident. They filed grievances every time possible.

As the agitation got stronger, the manager got more desperate in her attempts to get rid of black workers. Finally she made a mistake even Kroger could not ignore. To make some workers look bad, she forged a customer comment card with a complaint.

She got caught and was fired. And the workers came out stronger, because they had done it together.

#36

PRACTICE, PRACTICE, PRACTICE... DEBRIEF, DEBRIEF, DEBRIEF

No matter how well planned your campaign, you'll find that organizing is full of unexpected developments and unfamiliar experiences. Whenever you can, practice what you're about to do in a group, and debrief what you just did.

For instance, if you're planning to march on the boss to deliver a petition, definitely role-play it first, with the whole group if possible. Someone who likes to ham it up can play the boss. Try it a few times with different scenarios:

- Boss accepts your petition and says he'll get back to you.
- Boss shouts you down.
- Boss offers to meet privately with one or two people.
- Boss calls the cops.
- Secretary claims the boss isn't in.

Talk about how to react in each case. Agree on the order of speakers, and make sure everyone knows in advance what they're going to say. It's more effective if the known "troublemakers" hold back and let others do the talking, to show that this is an issue everyone cares about.

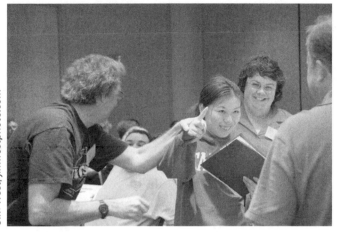

Jim West, jimwestphoto.com

Immediately after the action, re-group for a few minutes someplace nearby, such as in the parking lot. Ask "How do you think that went?" People may be thrilled—or disappointed, alarmed, or confused.

Talk about how to react in each case.

The organizer's role is to help interpret whatever just happened, and provide hope. Reassure people that the message was delivered, and make sure everyone feels good about what they did. Put management's reaction in the context of their known strategies (fear, hopelessness, confusion, division). Remind your co-workers how this action fits into your overall plan to win.

Your committee should meet regularly and role-play the one-on-one conversations you're having, too. Debrief your trouble spots. Work on answers to the tough questions that are stumping you.

#37

COUNT NOSES

At any given moment, your group's power depends on how many people you can move to action. So assess, reassess, and re-reassess your support.

Your power depends on how many people you can move to action.

Count your petition signatures. Keep track of how many people wear your buttons, stickers, or T-shirts. Have a sign-in sheet at the informational picket. At each step, is a larger percentage of your co-workers getting involved?

Keep updating your workplace map or chart from Lesson 3. Revisit your leader identification, especially in areas or among groups where participation is weak. Who else might have influence there? Who can influence the influencer?

Always be listening: What's the buzz? Did people like the last action? What's the scuttlebutt from management? What are people coming up with on their own?

UPDATE YOUR CHART

Remember the workplace chart you made in Lesson 3? It's a vital tool for tracking your progress on any campaign. Depending on your goals, your chart might include:

- Every member: name, location, shift, job title
- Union membership status
- Who's new
- Phone tree information
- Who's a steward
- Who signed up or recruited a member
- Who attended a training
- Who's on a contract action team

Charts are only as useful as they are accurate. Organizers should continually update their charts, and enlist co-workers to help. This can include tracking down people you didn't even know were members and removing those who have quit, gone on leave, or changed assignments.

Download this at
*labornotes.org/
secrets*

TEACHERS RAISE THE BAR

Sarah Jane Rhee, *loveandstrugglephotos.com*

The Chicago teachers, in their 2012 contract campaign, became masters at counting—they had to.

A state law had passed in 2011 requiring CTU to get yes votes from 75 percent of all members (not just those voting) before calling a strike. This was supposed to be impossible. "In effect they wouldn't have the ability to strike," gloated Jonah Edelman, an anti-union lobbyist who pushed for the rule.

CTU leaders were convinced that 75 percent was possible—but no one could deny it was a tall order. They couldn't go into the vote cold.

So activists tallied co-workers' participation in a series of activities—wearing red on Fridays,

HOW TO JUMP-START YOUR UNION

LESSONS FROM THE CHICAGO TEACHERS

A LABOR NOTES BOOK

Read more in *How to Jump-Start Your Union.*

signing an open letter, participating in a mock strike vote, and attending a citywide rally—all "tests we created for ourselves," as Staff Coordinator Jackson Potter put it.

They hung charts on the union office wall to keep track of every school and every delegate (steward). "We did a lot of counting," said Organizing Director Norine Gutekansl.

At the union's spring training conference, contract committee members went through the members at their schools name by name—assessing whether each person was wearing red, would come to an action, and would vote yes for strike authorization.

These assessments weren't considered permanent truths. The point of finding out where each person stood *now* was to aid an ongoing process of moving them closer to the center of the bullseye (see Lesson 1).

"Assessments were moving targets," said organizer Matthew Luskin. "The job of the delegate was to have a plan on how to move people. We offered them skills about how to overcome obstacles. It was empowering to people to realize that they could build support with these skills, rather than just lament the places it was missing."

By spring, CTU was passing its own tests with flying colors. The union was ready for the contract campaign's biggest hurdle, the strike vote. The teachers sailed over it, winning a 90 percent yes vote, and struck with nearly unanimous participation.

PERCEPTION CAN TRUMP REALITY

The battle for hearts and minds is crucial.

After your campaign is over, the battle for hearts and minds is crucial.

"In every battle there are at least two battles: what happened and what people think happened," says Jeff Crosby, the longtime president of IUE-CWA Local 201 at a General Electric plant in Lynn, Massachusetts.

"GE workers went on strike nationally for 101 days in 1969. The average member will tell you we gained nothing but a nickel. But in fact we got a number of substantial improvements, and we got better settlements for the next 30 years because of that strike—we convinced the company not to push us to a strike again.

"The same thing happened in '86. We had a local strike for four weeks which improved the discipline system and got them to stop harassing and firing stewards. The grievance procedure has worked better ever since then. But the leadership at the time didn't educate people on what they'd accomplished, so most people felt the 'respect strike' wasn't worth it."

After every battle with management, your bosses will very consciously spread their own version of

Massachusetts Uniting

what happened. You are fighting an uphill battle for people to believe they can win anything at all.

"It's not just the company," Crosby says, "but the dead weight of cynicism about everything in our society. People think 'the government sucks, the company sucks, politicians suck, the union sucks, of course we can't get anything, because we suck.' And there's always 'they're going to do what they want to do anyway.'"

When people default to believing the boss's version of events, they'll decide the struggle wasn't worth it— and that will make them hesitant to step up in the future.

> What people think happened is as important as what really happened.

"What we've tried to learn in our local," Crosby says, "is that you have to wage the second campaign as aggressively as the first one."

To wage the campaign over "what people think happened," talk one on one and in shop floor meetings that you call just for this purpose. Don't leave such discussions to the union meeting, which most members won't attend.

Emphasize what you won.

Emphasize what you won—even if it's just "we all stood together for the first time." That's important! Talk about how to make the most of what you won, stressing that any agreement with management is only as real as members make it on the job.

Spend a lot of time listening to what went right and wrong in the campaign. Brainstorm about what can be done differently next time, and think ahead about when to get started.

Has your campaign won an improvement yet? Congratulations! Savor it—while you can.

Even after a victory, you can never rest on your laurels. Management will always be looking to gain the upper hand and take away whatever you've won.

So in **Lesson 7: Always Be Organizing**, we'll learn how to keep organization going over time, so that an atmosphere of respect for workers becomes ingrained in the workplace. Warning: it takes a lot of maintenance.

LESSON 7: ALWAYS BE ORGANIZING

We hope you've taken a brcak while reading this book to go out and put the lessons into practice. Maybe you've gotten a few co-workers together, planned an action, even made your employer give in. Feels good, doesn't it?

But we know that bosses can be pretty relentless. *Their* bosses force them to be. You can be sure they'll be back tomorrow with more harassment or stupid rules. How can you create an atmosphere in the workplace that makes it hard for supervisors to bully and easy for workers to enforce fair standards?

For that, you need a group that stays in touch in between fights. Remember the bullseye model we discussed in Lesson 1? You need a core group and a circle of volunteers who are willing to do something when the need arises.

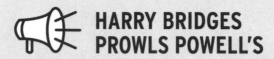

HARRY BRIDGES PROWLS POWELL'S

"Harry Bridges works at Powell's Books in Portland, Oregon," reports Michael Ames Connor. "He keeps an eye out for fellow workers. At least, that's what they say.

"The story, repeated by members of the West Coast Longshore union (ILWU), goes something like this: Every once in a while, over the store intercom, comes a page for Harry Bridges. 'Harry Bridges to the front register.' 'Harry Bridges to the loading dock.'

"These union folks who work at Powell's know that Harry has been dead for years. But they know his reputation—a fierce ILWU fighter who led the 1934 longshore strike that established the union. Part of joining ILWU means learning about their union, and learning what Harry Bridges stands for. They know that if he's going to check out the loading dock, they should, too.

When 30 or 40 people show up, the manager backs down.

"When they get there (and it's usually 30 or 40 people who show up), they find one of their co-workers in a little difficulty with the boss. A disagreement, an argument, a confrontation. Before they show up, maybe the boss is taking a hard line, getting ready to make an example of someone, thinking about tossing a troublemaker out the door. That's why Harry Bridges gets the call.

"So 30 or 40 people show up, and the manager backs down. Happens every time. With one or two people there, the boss can do what he likes. But with 30 or 40 people, as Arlo Guthrie once pointed out, you got yourself a movement.

"Nobody's ever seen Harry Bridges at Powell's. They just know he's there, watching to make sure nobody gets picked on, or picked off."

Sarah Race

#39

A LITTLE STRUCTURE GOES A LONG WAY

The key is to build enough structure for the issues you're dealing with.

The Powell's story shows a workplace culture where solidarity is the norm—using a system of communication that's simple yet powerful.

You may not need anything complicated where you work. The key is to build enough structure for the issues you're dealing with. There's no reason to have a parliamentarian and a sergeant-at-arms for a meeting of five or 10, but you will need a chair.

A regular lunch get-together in the cafeteria, or a meeting after work for a beer, may be all you need. Or you may need to build an official stewards council. Whatever the size, successful organization requires:

- **Communication**. It can be informal—a conversation at work or over coffee—or more formal, through a member-to-member network, where each person is assigned certain co-workers to talk with. Communication can include newsletters, leaflets, and social media, but it has to prioritize one-on-one, face-to-face conversations.

- **Accountability.** Activists know they can count on each other. They follow through and do what they said they would do when they said they would do it.

- **Solidarity.** An injury to one is an injury to all. Solidarity is built by being considerate and helpful to each other, rejecting favoritism, focusing on what we have in common, and developing a sense of family among co-workers.

POWER IS THE GOAL

For a group of workers to have collective power on the job, they need participation on three levels:

1. One or more **leaders** who put thought into what's happening at work, speak up, and propose action.

2. A normally small **group of co-workers** who work with and assist the leaders.

3. The support of **most or all of the rest** of the work group.

#40

SOCIALIZE TO ORGANIZE

Community Farmworker Alliance

"You can't expect people to march in the streets together if they don't even know each other's names," says Adam Heenan of the Chicago Teachers Union. As a union delegate (steward), he sees it as part of his job to help members at his school get to know each other.

"My thing has always been 'socialize to organize to mobilize,'" Heenan said.

This is not new advice. Since workers began to organize, they've been meeting at the bar after work or at the coffee shop beforehand. In the days when workers were more likely to live in the same neighborhood, near their workplace, and have ethnic clubs, social clubs, or churches in common, it was easier to bring people together outside work.

Today, we live farther apart and our commutes can be long. Because our lives are so busy, we often bolt for home the minute the whistle blows. Still, it's important to get together away from the supervisor's prying eyes, even if it's just for lunch during the workday.

Often it's conversations about our lives away from work that cement our respect for each other as human beings, and build the loyalty we need to stick together.

In Heenan's case, he went to a union caucus meeting, held at a deli, before he ever went to an official union meeting. "We ordered food and talked about issues," Heenan said. "I was surprised by the way everyone let each other talk and gave their opinions." The Caucus of Rank-and-File Educators was also doing movie screenings and running a reading group—plenty of chances for people to get to know each other and get involved on whatever level they chose.

'You can't expect people to march in the streets together if they don't even know each other's names.'

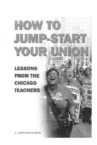

Read more in *How to Jump-Start Your Union*.

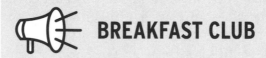

BREAKFAST CLUB

At UPS in Columbus, Ohio, a breakfast club helped part-time workers organize.

Nick Perry worked in the wee hours to sort packages by zip code and place them onto UPS's big brown trucks. "Our shift ends at 9 a.m. and we found ourselves talking in the building till 10:30," Perry remembers. "That naturally grew into going out to eat. We weren't thinking of organizing at first, it was more just empathy—venting and getting advice.

"So every Friday we would go out to breakfast and talk about what was going on at work, how to confront the supervisors who saw their job as constantly speeding us up. It started with four people and grew to nine. The managers started to notice and make fun of us, so we knew it was working."

'People felt way more confident than they ever had.'

Sorters were expected to lift 1,800 to 2,200 packages per hour, and the conveyor belt frequently got overloaded, with packages falling every which way. Workers had the right to stop the belt for safety, but most were afraid to exercise this right.

"The people who wanted to stop the belt were those who went to the Breakfast Club," said Perry. "People did, and found out they could get away with it, and that gave people more courage."

They started keeping a tally of how many times each worker cut off the belt. Workers would high-five whoever turned it off the most.

When Perry was moved to the late afternoon shift, he started a "wings club," where workers went out for wings after work. "We also started buying food and brought it in and shared it for our 10-minute break," he said, "and that really pissed management off.

"We went from cutting off the belt, to having members call OSHA, to filing Labor Board charges. People felt way more confident than they ever had."

THE MEETING BEFORE THE MEETING

Another breakfast club operated in a Seattle Plumbers and Pipefitters local. This one was formed by black workers who were facing discrimination from their local and from their fellow members. Eventually it grew to welcome other workers of color and women.

This club met on Saturdays before the monthly union meeting. When one of the members wanted to bring something up at the union meeting, the group would discuss it and get others' ideas and help, "so you're not just standing there by yourself," as one member put it.

The club also campaigned to get people into apprenticeships, to defend affirmative action in the state, and for union office.

#41

EVERYONE SHOULD BE PLUGGED IN

No one should be far from someone who's in the know.

You may not have access to an intercom like the one at Powell's Books. But you can figure out a way to set up your own word-of-mouth "intercom"—like a phone tree, but in person—to keep folks in regular touch with each other and with union activities.

You might organize it as a member-to-member network or as a small committee in each work area. The exact structure doesn't matter. The important thing is to have a dense web of organization, so that no worker is far from someone who's in the know.

MEMBER-TO-MEMBER NETWORK

A member-to-member network is made up of volunteers who commit to talking with certain co-workers, both on a regular basis and when the network is "activated."

Ideally, each volunteer should be responsible for no more than 10 co-workers. Fewer is better—it makes the job easier and gets more people involved. Build on the networks that already exist, including social ties and people who see each other at work.

You also need a handful of network coordinators, who stay in touch with the volunteers and meet

Chicago Teachers Union

regularly. Information from the coordinators can be
disseminated quickly to the entire workforce, almost
as fast as over an intercom.

Information should flow from the bottom up,
too. Coordinators should use the network to seek
feedback: How is the new system for transfers
working? Has the night-shift supervisor shaped up?

Volunteers should be proactive about asking co-
workers for their concerns, and passing that info to the
coordinators: "Everyone wants to know
why we gave $1,000 to the candidate for
sheriff."

Your activist network should complement the steward structure. Stewards
might make natural coordinators, or it
might work better to recruit different
members for the job. In any case, the network must work hand in glove with the
stewards. Avoid turf wars.

Read more in
*The Steward's
Toolbox.*

SECRETS OF A SUCCESSFUL ORGANIZER

MINI-COMMITTEE

Another approach is to form a "union committee" of two or more stewards or activists for a work area, who keep everyone else in the loop. Your committee should have regular meetings, plus the occasional on-the-fly meeting when a crisis comes up.

> **Committee members should be elected or confirmed in a democratic way.**

Committee members should be elected or confirmed in a democratic way. A California Service Employees local used a Steward Support Petition. "Anyone who wanted to be a steward had to get a majority in their work area to sign," wrote organizer Paul Krehbiel. "We wanted as many stewards as we could get, no limits. A work area with 25 workers and three stewards is stronger than an area with just one steward."

If the contract limits the number of stewards, that doesn't stop workers from also electing informal alternate stewards or committee members. This network can protect the steward from retaliation and make the workload more manageable.

"Many people who would like to become a steward don't do so because they fear the burden will fall on their shoulders alone," Krehbiel wrote. "When a group of people assumes a leadership role, the group generally comes up with better and bolder ideas, and feels they have the strength and support to carry them out."

EXERCISE:
SKETCH OUT A MEMBER NETWORK

Go back to your workplace map from Lesson 3. Can you start to see who would make good volunteers and who their assigned contacts would be? Think of the natural leaders, and of people who could be brought along with some training. Consider how to cover all the work groups and social groups.

Make up a first draft of a member-to-member network for your department or workplace. It's only a draft, of course. You will need to do the slow work of getting buy-in from the volunteers, and they will have their own ideas of who they want to stay in touch with.

Download this at
labornotes.org/secrets

📣 KEEP IT GOING

AFSCME Local 3299

A member-to-member network is often cemented during a contract fight. But don't let it wither away afterward! The structure needs to be continually and immediately available.

Put the network structure up on a wall chart or track it in a spreadsheet. Continually check to make sure no members have dropped out, and replace them if they have.

At the University of California campuses and hospitals, blue-collar workers with AFSCME Local 3299 expanded their Member Action Teams through a 2012 contract fight.

Organizers began with one-on-one conversations to identify the people most respected by their co-workers. They got to know these leaders by learning their stories and motivations. "We all have different reasons why we're involved," said Monica De Leon, a unit secretary. "This organizing is personal."

The organizers asked potential MAT leaders to:

- Bring co-workers to a picket or a departmental meeting, showing that their co-workers would follow their lead.

- Sign a pledge committing to the work of a MAT leader.

- Ask their co-workers to sign a pledge, too, to join in actions like picketing to win a good contract.

In less than a year, the union identified and recruited a battalion of new MAT leaders, bringing the total from fewer than 200 to 600. And most stayed active after the contract campaign was past.

"They are driving the workplace fights, defending the contract, and identifying other leaders of the union," said President Kathryn Lybarger. They're also tasked with signing up non-members.

The structure needs to be continually and immediately available.

MANY HANDS MAKE LIGHT WORK

"Those of us in the Heat and Ventilation Department at Massachusetts Institute of Technology had a problem," writes Paul McCafferty. "Our Service Employees shop steward, an experienced worker of 20 years, was resigning.

"No one was immediately interested in the job. A steward had a lot of stress, had neither super-seniority nor dues reduction, and could make enemies with both management and co-workers." It didn't help that the 35 workers were spread across three shifts, seven days, and six supervisors.

"A group of us came up with the idea of a shared, rotating stewardship. The idea was that four of us would share the steward position. We would each stand a three-month watch, and after a year we'd see how it had worked.

"We wrote up this idea, along with the names of the volunteers, posted it over the time clock, and asked our co-workers to sign the sheet as an endorsement. The majority signed, and we got the support of our business agent. Soon the four of us were armed with grievance forms, a new system, and no experience."

'The idea was that four of us would share the steward position.'

Over the next three years, eight people served three-month steward terms. (Some volunteered more than once.)

"The most important change we saw," McCafferty says, "was that the union was viewed less as an insurance plan, and more as something that we all had to make work. Because eight of us had processed grievances, there was a more widespread understanding of the strengths and weaknesses of the grievance procedure.

"The biggest drawback to rotation is that a new steward, by definition, has little experience. So mistakes can be made. But beyond the first step in a grievance, the business agent is present. This is

'The union was viewed less as an insurance plan.'

a big help to new stewards. And because there is a growing pool of present or former stewards, it's easy to get advice informally. Each year, as more workers get involved, more grievances are settled with the immediate supervisor.

"The biggest advantage of rotation is that it offers a manageable way for workers to get involved in the union. A commitment is required, but it's limited.

"In short, more hands, less work. More involvement, less burnout."

#43

CREATE A CONVERSATION-STARTER

Over the years, shop floor newsletters and leaflets have been great organizing tools. These days many organizers use email lists and Facebook groups for a similar purpose.

> Your publication is only as good as the real-life conversations it starts among co-workers.

But remember, whether you're using paper or pixels—it's a tool for organizing, not a substitute. Your publication is only as good as the real-life conversations it starts among co-workers and the action it provokes at work, where your power is.

The introverts among us may be tempted to just leave a stack of flyers on the break room table, or post a link on Facebook, and call that organizing. These shortcuts won't get you far.

Instead, an organizer should see every article, meme, status update, or newsletter as a prompt to start conversations like the ones you read about in Lesson 2.

When doing a survey, for instance, don't just hand them out. Offer to sit with the person and answer any questions as he or she fills it out. Even better, hold a "survey day" where everyone fills them out at the same time. That starts discussions.

WHAT A LEAFLET CAN DO

- **Create an opportunity for conversations.** "Hey, have you seen this? What do you think?"

- **Direct attention to your issue.** Especially when one co-worker sees another reading your leaflet, it can get people talking.

- **Create a distribution network.** The idea is for information to flow in all directions along this network, not just top-down from Leaflet Central.

MAKING THE BOSS LOOK RIDICULOUS

Michael Gould-Wartofsky

'We forced them to back down by raising so much hell at the worksite.'

Union contracts often include the right to a bulletin board in the workplace. Some are pretty drab—a faded union meeting notice from last year locked in a glass cabinet, next to a candy wrapper someone stuck through the cracks. But one union uses its bulletin boards to deflate management's credibility.

When state workers in New Jersey are involved in a fight, says Hetty Rosenstein, "we strip the bulletin board and turn it into a billboard," perhaps just a short slogan in huge letters. "It's amazing the impact this has," she says. "Management can't take it."

When one department was trying to eliminate seniority, Rosenstein recalls, "the union put up a picture of the department commissioner, but we made his head into a garbage can and showed job security being tossed into his head.

"It caused a huge furor. The top brass sent out notices to managers all over the state to take down pictures where the commissioner was a garbage can. They'd take down the pictures, and we'd put up another one, equally inflammatory.

"We grieved it and eventually won—the arbitrator said we had broad latitude to use our bulletin boards. And we forced them to back down on the seniority issue by raising so much hell at the worksite.

"I'm a great believer in ridicule. It debunks them and makes them seem less strong. It's easier to stand up to somebody who's ludicrous."

WHY MAKE A NEWSLETTER?

Bernard Pollack (CC BY 2.0) bit.ly/1L4eRV6

Even in a social media-dominated world, a regular print newsletter can be a visible expression of the union's power in the workplace. People see that they're not alone in questioning management's authority. One worker turns to another and says, "Hey, get a load of this!"

Bringing bosses' actions into the light of day puts pressure on management.

Bringing bosses' actions into the light of day puts pressure on management, too. You can tell by the way they overreact to the printed word.

The newsletter can chew out management, inform workers about what's happening in other departments and in the outside world, and offer criticisms and proposals to the union. It can also be the voice of a caucus. In a local that's very badly run, a rank-and-file newsletter can be one of the only ways that members find out what's going on.

A newsletter creates jobs for people with different sorts of skills—gathering news, writing, editing, cartooning, taking photos, designing, laying out, distributing, and fundraising. The more people involved, the stronger your credibility and base of support.

The more people involved, the stronger your credibility and base of support.

Anonymous newsletters have less credibility. Some newsletter groups, rather than putting a signature on each article, print a list of the names of everyone involved, to show that the newsletter is a collective product.

Download this at
*labornotes.org/
secrets*

GIVE PEOPLE THE INFO THEY WANT

Before the Caucus of Rank-and-File Educators won leadership of the Chicago Teachers Union, the group began publishing a monthly newsletter.

Each new issue was distributed at the monthly delegates (stewards) meeting. It featured news of forums and rallies the caucus was organizing, on issues union officers were ignoring. People started asking for bundles to hand out to everyone in their schools.

"At that time the union newsletter was big and glossy, with lots of pictures of the officers," said Kenzo Shibata, who ran communications for the caucus. "We just did a four-pager, with information on what was going on in the schools—and more people were reading our newsletter than were reading the official magazine."

'More people were reading our newsletter than were reading the official magazine.'

The caucus also had a busy email list and a blog displaying its many activities—again in stark contrast to the union's stale official website.

DEFEND YOUR RIGHTS

John Zartman of Teamsters Local 355 in Baltimore, a member of Teamsters for a Democratic Union (TDU), helped put out the *355 Informer*. The four-page newsletter regularly included a cartoon, a witty saying, columns with news from the different departments, and information on union rights.

The local leadership didn't react well. The president made several threats against the people putting out the *Informer*—but the activists knew they were protected against union retaliation by their International's constitution, federal labor law, and the First Amendment.

"We sent a letter saying we were not going to stop doing this," Zartman said. "I personally asked everyone involved in the newsletter, in writing, distributing, or whatever, if they wanted to sign the letter. Thirteen people put their names down."

TDU membership boomed, and there were other results, too. "We got a new business agent," Zartman said. "When we were getting ready to go into contract negotiations, the business agents wanted to know if they could submit an article to our newsletter."

TAKING THE CONVERSATION ONLINE

Here are a few ways organizers have used online tools:

VIRTUAL BREAK ROOM

An email list or Facebook group can be a forum to discuss issues, share information, draw up plans, and make contacts—off the clock and away from the boss.

Fast food workers at the Oregon Zoo communicated through a secret Facebook page when they organized to join Laborers Local 483. The online activities complemented an energetic on-the-job campaign that forged "zoolidarity" through actions such as a march on the boss.

Zoo workers used Facebook to complement an energetic on-the-job campaign.

"The Facebook page allowed us to answer questions about unions, address gossip at the zoo, announce organizing meetings, and later to respond to anti-union rumors that crept into the workplace," said Matt Ellison, part of the organizing committee.

Laborers Local 483

CONNECTING ISOLATED WORKERS

Email and Facebook can allow information-sharing and discussion among people who don't regularly see each other on the job.

Educators at California Virtual Academies, who work from home teaching online classes, used three Facebook groups to communicate during their organizing drive. One group, the "CAVA Water Cooler," offered a place to socialize, share stories, and vent. The second group was for supporters. The third was a private meeting space for the organizing committee to plan.

'Nothing's going to replace actually seeing each other.'

The 40-person committee also met regularly through a videoconferencing app called Zoom. But the educators met in person several times, too. "Nothing's going to replace actually seeing each other," said member Cara Bryant.

NETWORKING BETWEEN LOCALS

After teacher locals in a northern corner of Washington state organized one-day strikes against school underfunding, the "Badass Teachers" Facebook page helped the activity go viral. Soon, locals representing half the teachers in the state joined the strike wave.

Fired Portuguese dockworkers used Facebook to make contact even across national borders. Dockworkers in Spain turned away a ship loaded by scabs in Portugal—a crucial pressure point that helped the fired workers win back their jobs.

RANK-AND-FILE RESISTANCE

Machinists Local 751 member Shannon Ryker started the "Rosie's Machinists 751" Facebook page to rally Boeing workers against mid-contract concessions their International was pushing. Though the contract narrowly passed, the page became the seed for a new caucus.

Union dissidents such as rail workers, auto workers, and carhaulers stay in touch through email lists, conference calls, Facebook groups, and occasional in-person meetings. These methods helped Chrysler workers pull off a 2-to-1 "no" vote on their national contract in 2015, forcing bargainers back to the table to make improvements.

Judy Wraight

FACEBOOK TYPES

Page: Anyone can read, like, share, and comment on posts, but only the page owner can publish them. You might use this for official announcements from your union or campaign.

Public Group: Anyone can find, read, and join. You might use this for general conversation among members—but be aware the boss may be reading along.

Closed Group: Anyone can view the group's title and members, but only approved members can read the posts.

Secret Group: Members must be invited; the group doesn't show up in a search. Use this type of page to discuss contract negotiations or an organizing drive still under wraps.

Download this at
*labornotes.org/
secrets*

PORTRAIT OF A WELL-ORGANIZED WORKPLACE

Leaders in one nurses union drew up this list to illustrate their vision of an ideal, well-organized workplace:

The union is visible daily in the workplace to members and management.

1. Stewards or union volunteers make regular walk-throughs and have relationships with all members, not just elected leaders.

2. There is a steward or union volunteer on every shift, in every department. The list is written down, regularly updated, and widely available.

3. Membership meetings are regular and well-attended.

4. A union representative attends every new-employee orientation.

5. There is regular communication through newsletters, flyers, up-to-date bulletin boards, and a member-to-member network.

We defend our standards and enforce our contracts.

6. Members mobilize and use collective action to solve everyday problems. Grievances are not our primary line of defense.

7. Contracts are widely available and promptly distributed, both electronically and in print.

8. Stewards are trained and empowered to resolve issues at the lowest level, including filing grievances.

9. Managers do not act unilaterally or abusively, because they know they will get blowback.

Members own the union.

10. Members feel that their union is strong and can resolve problems.

11. Through stewards, members have immediate access to resources to resolve their problems, without having to track down the union rep.

12. Members participate in union-wide programs and campaigns.

13. Members are glad they belong to the union. Social events are well-attended.

Adapted from New York State Nurses Association

Download this at
*labornotes.org/
secrets*

EXERCISE:
GIVE YOUR WORKPLACE A CHECKUP

Look back over the list "Portrait of a Well-Organized Workplace." Assess the current state of your workplace for each item. Use this scale:

A   The statement is very true of your workplace.

B   It's mostly true.

C   It's somewhat true, in some areas.

D   It's barely true, or not true at all.

If you got some As and Bs, congratulations! If not, you're taking a first step.

Browsing back through your answers, identify two or three items as medium-term goals, things you think you can achieve over the next year and want to focus on. Jot down specific steps you'll need to take to move toward these goals.

Also pick out a couple of items as longer-term goals, things that might describe your workplace a few years down the line if you keep organizing. Jot down some intermediate steps you'll need to take to move toward those goals.

Download this at
labornotes.org/secrets

Are you starting to get a feel for how work life could be different if union members were organized and powerful?

This book has taken you through a lot of ideas. Some may seem like common sense (and yet putting them into practice is not so common). Some ideas may be brand new—great! Lots of light bulbs going off.

In the final installment, **Lesson 8: Putting It All Together**, you'll read a few real-life stories that bring all the parts together. And to make it easier to remember and refer to later, we'll sum up the lessons for you.

LESSON 8: PUTTING IT ALL TOGETHER

You've learned a lot—how to have an organizing conversation, map your workplace, find leaders, choose an issue, build a campaign from start to finish, overcome obstacles, and keep your organizing going beyond a single campaign. We hope you're already well on your way.

In this final lesson, you'll read two real-life case studies that bring together most of the secrets of a successful organizer. We'll also sum up the first seven lessons of this course—and offer a few final secrets.

CASE STUDY #1: A UNION SCHOOL

Teachers at Kelvyn Park High School in Chicago have transformed their school into one where the whole staff feels the union is strong, members are unafraid to speak up, and leadership is shared.

"The union is very present," said longtime steward Jerry Skinner. "We have a history that everyone is aware of." That history includes 100 percent participation in the 2012 strike and many confrontations with difficult principals.

New staff learn about the union right away, because members have transformed their lunchroom into a union hall. The latest union newsletters and copies of *Labor Notes* are available. Newspaper articles about the union's activities at Kelvyn Park have been blown up and turned into

Chicago Teachers Union

posters to decorate the walls, along with mementos from the strike.

Members also have an email list, coordinated by the stewards (called delegates), where all members receive and can respond to organizing updates.

MORE PROBLEM-SOLVERS

In recent years the stewards have maintained a policy of "one and done." "Once your three-year term as lead delegate is up, you step down," Skinner said. That brings new people into the steward role.

"Instead of looking for the 'right person' to fill the position," Skinner said, "we find people will rise to the occasion. People will find they have abilities and skills they didn't know they had."

That's partly because they get lots of mentoring. Former stewards continue to contribute, and today teachers are as likely to go to former stewards for help as to current ones.

Leaders at Kelvyn Park do surveys to discover the most pressing issues, and have made potent use of petitions. Facing a hostile principal in 2010, more than 90 percent of tenured teachers signed a petition that went over her head to her boss.

At an ensuing meeting with the boss's representative, 65 teachers were prepared to describe specific problems, including all the ways the principal was failing students. The two stewards "couldn't have done it by ourselves," Skinner said.

"We couldn't have countered his arguments. We needed the special education teachers there. We needed science teachers there. All the teachers would give their precise individual expertise. When the official tried to argue that the school was adequately funded in one area of instruction, a literacy teacher would say, 'No, that's a different budget.'

"This was a watershed moment for our school," Skinner said, "in which the experience and expertise of the entire staff, not just that of a couple of leaders, was demonstrated to the bosses and to each other."

Eventually Kelvyn Park got a new principal. Before she was hired, her boss discussed the nomination with a teacher leader, to find out whether she worked well with the staff.

WITH PARENTS AND STUDENTS

Union members reinforce their workplace presence by allying with parents and students. Chicago public schools each have a Local School Council (made up of parents, students, community members, teachers, and the principal) that meets monthly to oversee operations.

Active union members ran for and won seats on the LSC. Other members often come to meetings to keep the LSC informed about their views, grievances, surveys, and petitions.

As a result, the LSC has become far bolder in calling for more resources and a safer school. In 2010, 150 students even staged a midday walkout demanding more teachers. The same year, two parents and their children went to a school board meeting to speak against the principal's defunding of extracurricular programs. They got the money back.

By keeping their school well organized and vigilant, in recent years teachers have:

- Gotten back $300,000 that a principal tried to return to the board.

- Restored full funding of athletics programs.

- Restored teachers' right to make as many photocopies as they need.

- Rehired an experienced dean to deal with discipline.

- Saved the jobs of two P.E. teachers and one art teacher.

- Forced the principal to redo the evaluations of several veteran and activist teachers who were targeted with lower performance ratings.

"The administration will ignore you if it can," Skinner said, "but if you consistently show you're not scared to stand up to the principal or their boss, you can get somewhere. We've created a culture where that's the norm."

Read more in *How to Jump-Start Your Union.*

CASE STUDY #1
DISCUSSION QUESTIONS

How are Kelvyn Park High School teachers using the secrets of successful organizers?

Lesson 1: Attitude Adjustment

- What are activists at Kelvyn Park doing to preempt fear, hopelessness, division, and confusion—and make an "organizing attitude" the norm?

- What steps are they taking to get many people involved, insuring that the workplace organizer doesn't act as a lone ranger?

Lesson 2: One-on-One Conversations

- Where is the union creating opportunities for one-on-one conversations?

Lesson 3: Map Your Workplace and Its Leaders

- When did it prove especially important to have different categories of workers on board?

- How are leaders organizing democratically, helping to nurture more activists?

Lesson 4: Choosing an Issue

- What are some of the widely and deeply felt issues the teachers have organized around?

- What underlying values were at stake?

- Which issues inspired allies outside the workforce to get involved?

Lesson 5: An Escalating Campaign

- What tactics have the teachers used? Where would you place them on the thermometer?

- Which weak spots in the system did they find? How did they translate those into power?

Lesson 6: Expect the Unexpected

- When confronting a bullying boss, how did the teachers reduce the risk of retaliation?

Lesson 7: Always Be Organizing

- What structures have the teachers set up to keep their organizing going?

Download this at
labornotes.org/secrets

CASE STUDY #2: AN INJURY TO ONE IS AN INJURY TO ALL

Managers often go after those who seem weak or disadvantaged. Gregg Shotwell tells how members at an auto parts plant in Coopersville, Michigan, protected one of their own.

"There was a woman in our department who had attention deficit disorder," says Shotwell. "It made it difficult for her to learn new tasks. She was often late. She was a thorn in management's side."

A supervisor wanted this worker—we'll call her Rosie—to learn a new machine. When Rosie had trouble, the supervisor disqualified her from the job and switched her to another one, which only made matters worse. She monitored Rosie with constant questioning and criticism.

"The supervisor picked on Rosie because she was less able to defend herself," says Shotwell. "It was cruel."

Everyone could see that she was being mistreated.

Rosie wasn't the most popular worker; she often got on other people's nerves as well. But everyone could see that she was being mistreated. Workers had nicknamed this supervisor "the Terminator."

A few weeks before Christmas, the boss accused Rosie of running scrap—producing bad parts—and fired her. The supervisor told Shotwell to run Rosie's machine, but he shut it off and refused. "This machine is running scrap," he told the Terminator. "I'm not going to get fired, too."

When she insisted, Shotwell told her, "Fine. I will run scrap under direct order, but get my committeeman [steward], because I have to get it documented that you ordered me to run a machine that is producing scrap."

Sure enough, the machine produced scrap. "I made sure of that."

YOU WANT QUALITY?

Next, Shotwell and his co-workers found a way to use the company's quality-control program.

Jim West, *jimwestphoto.com*

"We had something called Document 40, in which an employee can document a quality problem. This creates a paper trail, and management is afraid of documentation. Since the quality problem couldn't be resolved without the involvement of production workers, job setters, and the skilled trades, we had control."

The quality problem was contagious; soon other workers were experiencing problems with their machines. Job setters who were usually quite skilled at making adjustments and small repairs appeared stumped, so they called out skilled trades.

"We explained to tradespeople what was happening. Nothing got fixed," says Shotwell. "Production slowed to a trickle."

ON VACATION

Rosie's co-workers weren't satisfied, though. "The next thing we did," says Shotwell, "was take up a collection for Rosie. We wanted management to know that she's not fired, she's on vacation. She's going to be paid one way or another."

They demanded a meeting with the general foreman, who said he would meet with one or two members. Instead, all the workers packed the conference room, outnumbering the four managers. Production in the department stopped.

Workers took turns relating incidents of harassment they had witnessed, and chronic quality problems they'd seen management ignore: "Firing Rosie doesn't change a thing." "It doesn't solve the poor quality problems." "She's a scapegoat, not a solution."

"We let them know we would pursue the Doc 40 all the way to the top of the corporation," says Shotwell.

CIVIL RIGHTS INVESTIGATION

Next, people from the department went to the union meeting. The union reps were reluctant to defend Rosie, but her co-workers demanded a civil rights investigation for harassment.

So one by one, the civil rights chairman took every worker, engineer, and supervisor in the department off the floor into a private room to interview them.

Many people sacrificed.

Arthur Geroge

Read more in *A Troublemaker's Handbook 2*.

"We workers talked, and talked, and talked. We ate up time like popcorn," Shotwell says. Production suffered, the shop floor buzzed with excitement, and management grew more and more anxious.

Adding to the slowdown, union members refused overtime. The Christmas shutdown was approaching, the company needed the parts, and workers were saying, "No, if you can afford to fire somebody, then you must not need the parts very bad." Many people who usually liked overtime before Christmas made a sacrifice.

The workers took up a collection to buy red and black T-shirts. The front said, "Stop Harassment," and the back said, "An injury to one is an injury to all."

"One of the reasons this solidarity action was so successful was that a woman who is well liked and respected, Kathy Tellier, got involved," Shotwell says. "She had credibility. Women, I often find, are brave in these situations. They really understand harassment. Kathy helped to rally the troops, both men and women."

VICTORY

Under all this pressure, management relented. The company settled the grievance and brought Rosie back to work. "The supervisor had to go to 'charm school,'" Shotwell said, which acknowledged the problem and embarrassed the Terminator.

"The day Rosie returned to work, she was the only one, on all three shifts, who wasn't wearing a 'Stop Harassment' T-shirt. Management saw solid proof that we would not tolerate harassment and discrimination.

Faced with mounting pressure, management relented.

"I felt really proud to be part of this action. Many people who are not usually outspoken or active or confrontational stepped forward. As an instigator my part was easy. I only had to appeal to the goodness in people's hearts.

"Given time and a patient instructor, Rosie did learn the job she was originally disqualified from. And management learned a valuable lesson: workers rule when they work to rule."

CASE STUDY #2
DISCUSSION QUESTIONS

How did Coopersville auto parts workers use the secrets of successful organizers?

Lesson 1: Attitude Adjustment

• Remember the fundamental issue: power. What power did management have? What power did the auto workers have?

Lesson 2: One-on-One Conversations

• When and why were one-on-one conversations especially necessary in this campaign?

Lesson 3: Map Your Workplace and Its Leaders

• How did it help to get the natural leaders and the different categories of workers on board?

Lesson 4: Choosing an Issue

• What was the widely and deeply felt issue that inspired workers to join this campaign?

• What underlying values were at stake?

• What made the workers think their demand was winnable?

Lesson 5: An Escalating Campaign

- What tactics did the workers use? Where would you place them on the thermometer? Did they escalate their tactics over time?

- Which weak spots in the system did the workers find? How did they use them?

- How did the workers put pressure on their union officers?

Lesson 6: Expect the Unexpected

- What potential roadblocks did the workers come up against? How did they overcome them?

- What were the signs that showed the action was getting through to management?

Lesson 7: Always Be Organizing

- What steps did the workers take that left them better organized for the next time?

- What do you think of the principle of defending an unpopular co-worker?

Download this at
labornotes.org/secrets

#44 BE MILITANT, BUT BE SMART

James Leder

Although the National Labor Relations Act guarantees us the right to organize and take action at work, there are restrictions. For instance, refusing a direct order can get you into hot water. Unless you're prepared for the consequences, don't do it.

Instead, when the boss gives a direct order, try to discuss it with him. If he won't, smile and switch tactics.

"Stewards need to be militant but smart," write David Cohen and Judy Atkins. "They need to know how to bend the rules without getting their people in trouble."

Here are two examples of how to take (or not take) concerted action.

GOOD EXAMPLE: BATHROOM-LINE SOLIDARITY

The union at a tool plant was campaigning to end a wage freeze. To pressure the company, workers produced exactly as many parts as the contract required. Most had previously produced a lot more—and made more money—but now the company was receiving one-third less production.

At break and lunch times, up to 100 workers would line up at the bathrooms and the phones. (This was back in pre-cell-phone days.) When the break ended, there would still be long lines.

When supervisors intervened, workers would explain one by one why they needed to call home (sick kids, spouse emergency) or use the bathroom. If ordered personally, each would politely return to work. Some would soon get back in line with a new explanation.

These actions continued every day for six months, until the company agreed to reopen the contract.

WHAT DID THESE WORKERS DO RIGHT?

- They never risked discipline for insubordination. No one told a boss to go to hell or refused a direct order.

- Although participation was never 100 percent, workers didn't turn against each other.

BAD EXAMPLE: WHISTLING DOWN THE BOSS

Workers at a windows factory were furious over harassment. One day at lunch, the entire factory marched into the offices, blowing whistles and chanting.

Secretaries looked on in disbelief. The boss shouted an order to go back to work, but no one could hear him over the noise.

The lunch period ended. Soon the bosses began ordering workers back one by one. Some left, others stayed. Ten minutes later the remaining workers marched back to work.

The company fired 10 workers for insubordination —the ones who'd been last to leave the office. The union alleged retaliation for union activities, but the Labor Board ordered it to arbitration.

At the arbitration hearing, the union rep and some of the workers were hostile to the company and proud of what they'd done. The arbitrator did not react well. He admitted workers had a right to protest inside the factory while on lunch break.

But he singled out the union rep for preventing secretaries from working. Workers had overstayed their break and many had refused a direct order. He upheld the dismissals of three union leaders who had been last to leave the office (and the most macho in the hearing).

WHAT SHOULD THESE WORKERS HAVE DONE DIFFERENTLY?

- Not marched into an area where other workers would be disrupted.

- Obeyed direct orders, at least eventually.

- Kept a close eye on the clock and made sure everyone was back to work before lunch ended.

- Remembered who they were talking to in the arbitration hearing.

#45 YOU'RE GOING TO LOSE MORE OFTEN THAN YOU WIN

Milwaukee Teachers' Education Association

One hard reality about organizing: you're going to fail a lot. You'll lose more often than you win. This doesn't mean you're doing it wrong.

One action usually doesn't carry the day.

You'll start a lot of things that won't go anywhere. In fact, if that's not happening, it means you're not trying enough things.

One action usually doesn't carry the day; it takes persistence. And even a well-planned campaign, with a strong issue, good leaders, and escalating tactics, will often end in defeat. Scratch beneath the surface of any big victory, and you'll find it was preceded by a series of losses. You keep losing until you win.

Chin up. Learn everything you can from every loss. Find the silver linings, such as the new activists and supporters you recruited. Shore them up and build for the next time.

See each fight as a chance to practice playwright Samuel Beckett's advice: "Try again. Fail again. Fail better."

Learn everything you can from every loss.

REMEMBER THE BASICS

PASNAP

As you move through your organizing plan, keep these principles in mind:

TALK ONE ON ONE

Listen to what your co-workers are saying. Share your own ideas. Don't just gossip or gripe—help create a focus about problems that can be solved.

ENCOURAGE CONFIDENCE

You and your co-workers may feel scared or hopeless. A calm and confident attitude helps. Remind people what will happen if they do nothing. Help them draw on their righteous indignation instead of their fear.

CHALLENGE AUTHORITY

Organizers don't need to demonize the boss. We do need to encourage people to question authority and stand up for each other. Figure out how to confront the people in power.

Figure out how to confront the people in power.

RECRUIT GOOD LEADERS

Take note of who is naturally respected and encourage them to take on leadership. Look for each person's talents and find ways to use them. Don't let the whiners set the tone.

IDENTIFY COMMON PROBLEMS AND SHARED HOPES

We organize to bring people together. Talk and listen until you've found a problem that matters to lots of your co-workers. Share what you've heard.

ORGANIZE DEMOCRATICALLY

Include everyone who is, or might be, affected. Reach out beyond your friends and the people most like yourself. Solicit opinions and involve as many people as possible in decisions. Find a role for everyone.

SET CONCRETE GOALS

Goals should be specific. State clearly what a victory would be. Make sure the majority of people share this goal.

GET PEOPLE MOVING

Even simple collective activity is better than just talking. Action breeds commitment. Circulate a petition. Wear buttons. Develop plans that involve small steps. Each step should slowly increase the visibility and strength of the group.

STICK TOGETHER

As long as an action is collective, you won't leave individuals vulnerable. Design activity that brings people together. Send a group to talk to the boss. Write a letter that everyone signs.

Alexandra Bradbury

NO SHORTCUTS

Resist the temptation to do it all yourself, or to shoot out an email and consider your co-workers informed. Even if it seems inefficient at first, getting more people involved is the only way to keep things going over the long run.

TURN UP THE HEAT

Start with small actions that will probably succeed. With new confidence, people will be inspired to take bigger and riskier steps.

If you have a phone tree, you're on your way.

EVALUATE AS YOU GO

Keep talking one on one and in groups. Assess whether your goals are still correct and clear. Evaluate whether new plans are needed.

ORGANIZATION IS EVERYTHING

Your organization doesn't need to be too formal, but it does need to get the job done. If you have a phone tree, you're well on your way. Organize social get-togethers, too.

EYES ON THE PRIZE

Step back, look at the big picture, and don't let setbacks discourage you for long. Remember you're part of a much bigger movement. Pass the torch along to the next generation.

Download this at *labornotes.org/ secrets*

#46

FIND HOME BASE

Jim West, jimwestphoto.com

Every two years, thousands of us gather for the Labor Notes Conference. We come to sharpen our skills, meet new people, and talk strategy. But the biggest draw is the overwhelming feeling the event gives you—the feeling that you are not alone.

> **There's a reason they want us to feel isolated and powerless. It's because we're not.**

As Racine, Wisconsin, teacher Angelina Cruz put it: "There's a reason we're supposed to feel isolated and powerless. It's because we're not." It turns out you're part of a growing community of organizers who are serious about putting the *movement* back in the labor movement.

The conference is a tremendous resource for finding like-minded folks in your industry or union, and it's uplifting. For many workplace organizers, Labor Notes becomes both a lifeline and a home base.

If you've read this far, it's a good bet you share the basic values that unite us: You believe that the members *are* the union, and that they should be in the driver's seat. You think power is built from the bottom up, starting where we're strongest, on the job. You're fighting to improve members' day-to-day work lives—but you certainly don't stop there. You want to be part of a labor movement that can change the world.

> You're part of the 'troublemaking wing' of the labor movement.

Welcome home. You are part of the "trouble-making wing" of the labor movement—and Labor Notes is yours, too.

In between conferences, this remarkable community doesn't vanish. Here are five ways to stay in touch with fellow organizers and troublemakers:

1. Join our weekly email list at *labornotes.org*.

2. Connect through local Troublemakers Schools, one-day conferences held in cities around the country. See what's coming up at *labornotes.org/events*—and if there's not one near you, contact the Labor Notes office to find out how you can put one together.

Alexandra Bradbury

3. Subscribe to our monthly magazine, *Labor Notes*. It's packed with news you won't find anywhere else, including honest analysis of labor's latest victories and defeats, often written by the people on the front lines. Every issue features a "Steward's Corner" full of advice from experts and stories from organizers. When you have a story of your own to tell, write to *editor@labornotes.org*.

4. Go deeper with our other books. Lots of the lessons you've just read were drawn from *A Troublemaker's Handbook 2*, *The Steward's Toolbox*, *Democracy Is Power*, and *How to Jump-Start Your Union*, which have been manuals for thousands and thousands of union members. To find them all (and get a Troublemakers Union T-shirt), visit *labornotes.org/store*.

5. If your group is looking for tailored training or advice, Labor Notes can connect you with veteran organizers around the country. Fifty trainers and advisors are part of the Labor Notes Associates program, offering their expertise on topics ranging from steward basics to contract campaigns to what to do after you're elected to union office. We've worked with everyone from small caucuses to international unions. To find out how Labor Notes can help your group, email *training@labornotes.org*.

#47

ORGANIZE FOR THE LONG HAUL

Annette Bernhardt (CC BY-SA 2) bit.ly/1LTJOG8

You've been reading about thousands of people who are organizing with their co-workers to take control of their work lives. It's not easy. Our employers—and too often our elected officials—have been bearing down on us for decades. It's almost all we can do to hold our ground. But some have been able to push back.

We have the power to beat employers at their own game.

There's a lot we can learn from these troublemakers. First and foremost, when ordinary workers act together, we have the power to beat employers at their own game.

When you're doing the day-to-day work of an organizer—talking to your co-workers, passing out leaflets, going to another union's picket line—you can't always see how you fit into the big picture. You're too close.

But if you step back, you'll see that our movement is built on millions of little actions just like yours. They're all part of shifting the balance of power in our direction.

GRAINS OF SAND

In Mexico there's a saying, "*Traigo mi granito de arena.*" It means, "I bring my little grain of sand." Each of us brings our own little grain of sand to the project of building a better world.

What you are doing every day when you start that conversation at work, or circulate a group grievance, or show a co-worker it's okay to stand up to the supervisor, is adding your bit of grit.

No matter the frustrations, don't give up. We may lose a lot more than we win—but sometimes our victories change everything.

And although history is often recorded as the story of great men acting individually, we know that almost everything working people have ever won has been the result of thousands of ordinary folks acting together, with the courage to bring their own grains of sand.

EVERYDAY PEOPLE

Leaders like John L. Lewis, head of the Congress of Industrial Organizations, are often given credit for the great labor victories of the 1930s. But Lewis was propelled by the thousands of workers who risked their jobs to sit down in auto plants, steel mills, and Woolworth stores.

Movements emerge after years of spadework.

When we think of the civil rights movement, we think of Rosa Parks and Martin Luther King, Jr. But they were propelled by thousands of African American maids, field hands, factory workers, and teenagers who stood up to police dogs and fire hoses, together with thousands of allies of all races who believed in justice.

Those movements, and every other movement, were created by all the individuals who went up to someone else and said, "Let's *do something*."

THINGS CAN CHANGE QUICKLY

In 1937, more than 3 million workers joined the labor movement and close to 2 million went on strike. It seemed like things changed overnight.

But movements like that don't just emerge out of thin air. The ground had been prepared by years of spadework, by person after person bringing their grains of sand.

The labor upheaval of the 1930s was born out of decades of prior organizing. Activists from the Wobblies, the Farmer-Labor Party, and the old American Federation of Labor mixed in with radical immigrants and homegrown socialists on the shop floor. They developed reputations as trustworthy leaders.

Some of them kicked off the wave of strikes and organizing. Others were there to lead it when it spread to their factories.

The same thing is true of the civil rights movement of the 1960s. It grew out of long-term work by the NAACP, African American churches, and a host of community groups in both the North and the South.

Rosa Parks was not just a tired woman on a bus. She was a trained organizer, part of a group who had made a strategic decision to take on Jim Crow.

BE READY

That's the common denominator across the strike wave of the 1930s, the civil rights movement of the 1960s, and even the Occupy Wall Street movement a few years ago. When the opportunity presented itself, organizers were ready—and were willing to aim higher than anyone thought possible.

Dorret (CC BY 2.0) bit.ly/dorretphoto

Nothing fuels a movement like victory. After the Montgomery bus boycotters won in 1956, the civil rights movement spread like wildfire. When the winds shift, the little campaign we lead today can swell into a powerful movement tomorrow.

Chicago's example touched off a national wave of teacher, student, and parent activism.

The next upsurge will call for legions of skilled, far-sighted activists. We sharpen our skills by getting into fights, and hopefully winning some.

Convincing co-workers to have each other's backs against a common enemy is essential practice for the kind of organizing it takes to change the balance of power in our communities and our whole society.

LONG-DISTANCE RUNNERS

This book includes scores of tactics and strategies. They're not guaranteed to produce victory. Sometimes the employers are stronger than we are, and they win. Or we win a round, but it's only round one in a much longer fight.

Movements need long-distance runners. We have to be in it for the long haul.

It took activists in the Chicago Teachers Union years to transform their passive union into the fighting organization that pulled off a winning strike in 2012. And as electrifying as the strike was, it was only one chapter in a much longer story.

The year after the strike, the union's nemesis Mayor Rahm Emanuel slashed back, closing nearly 50 schools at once, the most any U.S. city had ever seen. As we write in 2016, the union is in the midst of its next intense contract campaign, battling attacks on teachers' pensions and preparing for another possible strike. Teachers and their community allies continue to inspire with brave hunger strikes and civil disobedience.

But the Chicago teachers have found that they're not alone. Their example touched off a national wave of teacher, student, and parent activism. Dozens of teacher unions have launched their own campaigns for "the schools students deserve." They've upped the ante by boycotting tests, working to rule, and conducting rolling strikes.

What keeps people going despite the reversals is the knowledge that you are part of something bigger than yourself. Folksinger Pete Seeger used to describe a giant seesaw. One end is weighed down by the rich and powerful. At the other end, activists are adding sand, one teaspoon at a time.

"One of these years, you'll see that whole seesaw go *zooop* in the other direction," Seeger said. "And people will say, 'Gee, how did it happen so suddenly?' Us and all our little teaspoons."

MORE LABOR NOTES BOOKS

A Troublemaker's Handbook 2: How to Fight Back Where You Work and Win!

This book explains how to take control of your life at work, using first-person accounts from ridiculing a pompous boss to beating a multinational corporation.

"*A Troublemaker's Handbook 2* is the best resource available to empower workers on the job. Every steward and activist at every worksite in the country should have a copy." —Paul Krehbiel, organizer

How to Jump-Start Your Union: Lessons from the Chicago Teachers

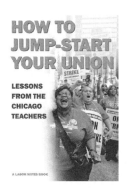

Discover how activists transformed their union from the bottom up and gave members hope. Learn how to run for office, work with your community, build a stewards network, train new leaders, run a contract campaign, and strike.

"It's a toolkit that shows how good old-fashioned hard work and faith in the membership can empower every frontline worker." —Karen Lewis, President, Chicago Teachers Union

The Steward's Toolbox: Skills and Strategies for Winning at Work

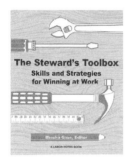

Shop floor activists are the raw material for labor's revival. Our movement needs thousands more stewards with the skills, confidence, and authority to stand up.

The Steward's Toolbox is a how-to resource guide, offering experience and advice on everything from how to defend past practices to how to build a coalition to defeat privatization.

Democracy Is Power: Rebuilding Unions from the Bottom Up

The missing element in many of today's debates about rebuilding the labor movement is internal democracy. This book shows what member control really looks like, and why it's crucial to labor's future.

The authors discuss everything from how to get an honest union election to what it looks like to build a democratic union culture. If you want to put members in the driver's seat, this book is for you.